D1616906

WOMEN IN NIGERIA

Recent Titles in
African Special Bibliographic Series

Population, Urbanization, and Rural Settlement in Ghana: A Bibliographic Survey
Joseph A. Sarfoh, compiler

African Women: A General Bibliography, 1976–1985
Davis A. Bullwinkle, compiler

Women of Northern, Western, and Central Africa: A Bibliography, 1976–1985
Davis A. Bullwinkle, compiler

Women of Eastern and Southern Africa: A Bibliography, 1976–1985
Davis A. Bullwinkle, compiler

The Press in Nigeria: An Annotated Bibliography
Chris W. Ogbondah, compiler

Health, Disease, Medicine and Famine in Ethiopia: A Bibliography
Helmut Kloos and Zein Ahmed Zein, compilers

African Music: A Bibliographical Guide to the Traditional, Popular, Art, and Liturgical Musics of Sub-Saharan Africa
John Gray

South Africa's Road to Change, 1987–1990: A Select and Annotated Bibliography
Jacqueline A. Kalley

Idi Amin and Uganda: An Annotated Bibliography
Martin Jamison, compiler

Energy in the Development of West Africa: A Selected Annotated Bibliography
Joseph A. Sarfoh, compiler

Family Planning and Reproductive Health Services in Ghana: An Annotated Bibliography
Yaw Oheneba-Sakyi, compiler

Metalworking in Africa South of the Sahara: An Annotated Bibliography
Ibironke O. Lawal, compiler

WOMEN IN NIGERIA

An Annotated Bibliography

Compiled by

UCHE AZIKIWE

African Special Bibliographic Series, Number 20

GREENWOOD PRESS
Westport, Connecticut • London

Library of Congress Cataloging-in-Publication Data

Azikiwe, Uche.
  Women in Nigeria : an annotated bibliography / compiled by Uche
Azikiwe.
    p. cm.—(African special bibliographic series, ISSN
  0749–2308 ; no. 20)
    Includes bibliographical references and indexes.
    ISBN 0–313–29960–9 (alk. paper)
    1. Women—Nigeria—Social conditions—Bibliography. 2. Women in
development—Nigeria—Bibliography. I. Title. II. Series.
  Z7964.N6A95   1996
  [HQ1815.5]
  016.3054′09669—dc20   95–47167

British Library Cataloguing in Publication Data is available.

Library of Congress Catalog Card Number: 95–47167
ISBN: 0–313–29960–9
ISSN: 0749–2308

First published in 1996

Greenwood Press, 88 Post Road West, Westport, CT 06881
An imprint of Greenwood Publishing Group, Inc.

Printed in the United States of America

The paper used in this book complies with the
Permanent Paper Standard issued by the National
Information Standards Organization (Z39.48–1984).

10 9 8 7 6 5 4 3 2 1

To my paternal and maternal grandmothers,
Uche Alu Inya and Mgbo Ebiya

Contents

Preface

Women's studies, which has hitherto been a neglected field of learning in Nigeria, is now becoming more popular and appreciated. There is therefore a need to document past works and create a bibliography to serve as a foundation for current and future studies and as a guide. This foundation will help to determine solutions to the innumerable problems constraining women in their struggle for emancipation. This book will also help in the efforts to improve the quality of lives of the womenfolk in Nigeria. This is in view of the fact that solutions to the constraints impeding effective participation of women in the development process will be difficult to come by unless the dimensions of the problems are known. This bibliography highlights some of the unknown problems, solutions to the problems, and numerous steps toward uplifting the status of the Nigerian woman. To the best of my knowledge, there is only one bibliography entirely on women in Nigeria by M. Kisekka. *Women in Nigeria: An Annotated Bibliography,* therefore, may be regarded as my humble contribution to the advancement of women's studies in Nigeria in particular and in the world at large. It has updated whatever has been done so far on documentation of data on Nigerian women.

I have assembled in this volume various materials from books, journals, theses, dissertations, government documents and conference papers available in the libraries and centres visited. Both published and unpublished materials on the Nigerian woman or girl from 1975 to 1993 were considered for inclusion. The UN Decade for Women launched in 1975 ignited the flame of interest in women's studies in the hearts of many. At the end of the decade, 1985, the call for data banks on women was made in every member country. This bibliography is a result of that call. Hence, the period covered in the project is from 1975. By starting from the first year of the decade I hope to reveal the effect of the UN programme on research on women's issues in Nigeria.

The libraries of the five premier universities in Nigeria at Ibadan, Nsukka, Lagos, Ife and Zaria were visited in the course of this study. Also visited were libraries of universities in nerarby Abia and Imo States, the Women's Documentation Centre at the University of Ibadan, and the British Council Library at Enugu. The newer university libraries were excluded primarily because students from these universities visit the oldest institutions' libraries for their research work. Secondly, official commitments restricted my travels to other nearby Universities.

It was not possible to include many 1993 publications in the compilation because most, if not all, Nigerian academic journals are not published when due. For instance, some new journals and other publications that were in circulation in 1994 are issues from as far back as 1991 and 1992. Nor, for the same reason, was it possible to cover 1994 and 1995. This situation is primarily a result of the present economic depression in Nigeria that has brought academic publishing and many publishing houses to a halt. Furthermore, the embargo on importation of books, as well as the high cost of importation when permitted, are other contributing factors. However, since the primary purpose of this bibliography is to compile what exists at the time of investigation, the absence of many 1993 publications makes no difference. There is no doubt that this book contains up-to-date and useful data on Nigerian women for the public, policy makers, and researchers. This is the main object of a bibliography. It is my belief that, in due course, other interested individuals will continue the documentation.

This bibliography contains 521 entries and has seven chapters made up of related works. The classification into various headings is not watertight. However, a close look at a chapter will reveal some degree of relatedness of theme.

Chapters 1 to 3 are on Agriculture and Economy, National Development, and Education and Training respectively. The next three chapters, 4 to 6, cover Health, Home and Family, and Labour Forces and Work Place. The last, chapter 7, is captioned General, and could also be said to be a potpourri because it contains many areas that have very few collections. Areas grouped under General are Women in the Media, Law, Novel, Politics, Women in Professions, and other bibliographies.

This book of reference, as stated earlier, is not claiming to have covered all possible areas or to contain all works on women in Nigeria for the period covered due to uncontrollable circumstances. Nevertheless, it is hoped that this annotated bibliography will provide some valuable data on women in this country and beyond. It is also hoped that as a reference book, it will be quite useful to readers, researchers, and planners interested in women in Nigeria, in particular, and women the world over.

Uche Azikiwe, Ph.D.
Institute of Education
University of Nigeria, Nsukka

Acknowledgements

This book owes its existence to the call by international and national bodies, non-governmental organisations, goverments, and individuals for documentation of materials on women in an effort to build up a data bank. The call was made in 1985 at the end of the United Nation's Decade for Women.

The main bulk of the materials were collected between 1985 and 1991 while I was conducting investigations for my M.Ed. thesis and Ph.D. dissertation.

I acknowledge my indebtedness to the following: Ohuche, R.O.; Nzewi, U. and Nwachukwu, V.C. (1988); Institute of Education, University of Nigeria, Nsukka (1991); Blackhurst, H. (1985-88); Boesch, P. (1987-98); Kisekka, M. (1981); and UNESCO (1983).

Last but not least, I thank all those whose words of encouragement helped to make this book a reality.

WOMEN IN NIGERIA

1

Agriculture and Economy

1. Adamu, Ladi (1978) Women and Farming. *Africa Woman*, November/December, p.44.

This paper treats the involvement of women in agriculture, highlights their problems, and concludes that more efforts should be made to incorporate more women into farming in Nigeria.

2. Adekanye, T.O. (ed.) (1988) *Women in Agriculture, African Notes-Journal of the Institute of African Studies*. Special Number 3. (WORDOC), Ibadan: University of Ibadan.

This volume contains the papers presented on "Women in Agriculture" at the Seminar on Nigerian Women and National Development organized by the Institute of African Studies, University of Ibadan, 20-21 June, 1985. The range of the thirteen papers in the volume is quite wide, and they are grouped into six categories: (1) Women in Agriculture; (2) The Role of Women in Agriculture in Nigeria; (3) Commodity Review and Division of Labour; (4) Food Processing; (5) Rural Poverty and Nutrition; and (6) Policies.

3. Adekanye, T.O. (1988) Women and Rural Poverty: Some Considerations from Nigeria. In T.O. Adekanye (ed.), *Women in Agriculture, African Notes: Journal of the Institute of African Studies,* Special No. 3, WORDOC University of Ibadan, 63-68.

This paper focuses on the poverty of women in African agriculture on the basis of a Nigerian case study. A short review of rural poverty is provided and the nature of women's poverty is discussed with particular reference to Nigeria. The policy implication of the case study for alleviating this poverty is that integrating study into development does not only mean involving them in rural imbalance projects. Rather, it means ensuring that initial imbalance entailed in low status, limited access to agricultural resources, heavy work load, low income, and so forth, for women, relative to men, is corrected.

4. Adekanye, T.O. (1987) African Women in Agriculture: Problems and Policies for Development. *Presence Africaine*, No. 141, 7-14.

The objective of this paper is to highlight and appraise the role of women in agriculture and in the rural economies of Africa in order to design appropriate policy measures for the use of women as a catalyst for agricultural development and rural transformation. A review of the activities of women in the agricultural economy of Nigeria, and their involvement in cooperation in agriculture are assessed to indicate the extent to which rural women are integrated into, or by-passed by rural development projects. Appropriate strategies are then discussed, on the basis of the Nigerian review.

5. Adeyemo, R.O. and Ajobo, O. (1988) Working Women in the Food Processing Industry: A Case Study in Lagos Area of Nigeria. In T.O. Adekanye (ed.), *Women in Agriculture, African Notes: Journal of the Institute of African Studies,* Special No. 3, WORDOC, University of Ibadan, 55-60.

This paper analyses women's involvement in the non-traditional food processing industry in Lagos and identifies such problems as male domination of top management positions; labour union's relative inactivity on maternity leave issues; and provision of day-care centres. Improved social infrastructures would help towards solving some of the women's problems.

6. Adeyeye, V.A. (1988) Women's Involvement in Agriculture and Rural Development. In T.O. Adekanye (ed.), *Women in Agriculture, African Notes: Journal of the Institute of African Studies,* Special No. 3, WORDOC, University of Ibadan, 17-22.

The author uses empirical data obtained from a case study undertaken in Oyo state of South Western Nigeria. On the basis of this, frequency distribution of the women's responses are presented to indicate the non-specific activities undertaken by the women, the crops grown by them, and the ranking of their socio-economic activities.

7. Adeyeye, V.A. (1980) Women in Traditional Agriculture: Oyo State of Nigeria Experience. *Unpublished M.Sc. Thesis*, Department of Agricultural Economics, Ibadan: University of Ibadan.

8. Adeyokunnu, T.O. (1980) *Women and Agriculture in Nigeria.* Study commissioned by the Training and Research Centre for Women of United Nations Economic Commission for Africa. Addis Ababa.

A survey of 600 rural women in the northern, eastern and western parts of Nigeria in 1978-79. The results reveal that trading was the most important activity outside the home, followed by farming. However, while the Ibo women of the Eastern Nigeria were mainly farmers and the Yoruba women of Western Nigeria were largely traders, the socio-economic activities of the Hausa women of Northern Nigeria in either farming or trade were severely restricted because of the moslem practice of keeping women in *purdah.*

9. Akande, S.O. and Igben, M.S. (1984) Intra-agricultural Inequality: The Male-Female Dichotomy. *Ife Social Sciences Review.* 7 (1 and 2), 215-235.

The authors examine inequality within the agricultural industry. The focus is on sex inequality, under the assumption that inequality exists between men and women in agriculture arising from structural imperfection in resource ownership and distribution, unequal access to opportunities, and from lack of infrastructural facilities.

10. Ayo-Bello, M.B. (1988) Cooperative Development for Women in Nigeria. In Linda Mayonk (ed.), *All are Not Equal: African Women in Cooperatives.* Report of a Conference held at the Institute for African Alternatives, 10-11 September 1988. London: IFAA, pp.61-62.

This paper looked at the level of participation of women in cooperatives in Nigeria. The author highlighted the inhibiting factors to women's equal participation, such as culture, literacy, inappropriateness of existing agricultural programmes, discrimination, and absence of women at the management and policy making levels. The advantages of women's participation in cooperatives were also discussed. Suggestions to increase women's participation in cooperatives included extension education, more female extension agents, channelling of inputs to women's cooperatives, and finance.

11. Babalola, A.S. (1988) Tobacco Farming and Women in Rural Community of Nigeria. In T.O. Adekanye (ed.), *Women in Agriculture, African Notes:*

Journal of the Institute of African Studies, Special No. 3, WORDOC, University of Ibadan, 39-44.

This paper examines tobacco farming and reveals that there are complementary roles for husbands and wives, with negative impact on women as they work for their husbands, although some benefits of their husbands improved financial position accrued to them. The study shows also that more tobacco farmers' wives now possess more independent occupations than before.

12. Ezumah, N. (1988) Women in Agriculture: Neglect of Women's Role. In T.O. Adekanye (ed.), *Women in Agriculture, African Notes: Journal of the Institute of African Studies,* Special No. 3, WORDOC, University of Ibadan, 9-16.

This paper starts with a review of the meaning of development, particularly as it relates to the notion of basic needs. Reviews previous studies and then draws some conclusions from a preliminary study of Igbo rural women of Eastern Nigeria.

13. Famoriyo, S. (1988) The Significance of Women in Nigerian Agriculture. In T.O. Adekanye (ed.), *Women in Agriculture, African Notes: Journal of the Institute of African Studies,* Special No. 3, WORDOC, University of Ibadan, 83-88.

This paper is on policy issue and suggests research documentation on Nigerian rural women; infrastructural improvement and training; formation of cooperative societies by women; and the incorporation of women's access to land into Nigeria's Land Use Act.

14. Fatunla, G.T. (1988) The Involvement of Women in Small-scale Food Processing and Distribution in Ondo State. Report submitted to the Social Science Council of Nigeria on the Food Foundation Supported Research on SS Food Processing and Distribution Industries in Nigeria.

15. Igbozurike, M. (1988) Nigerian Rural Women in Agricultural Development. In T.O. Adekanye (ed.), *Women in Agriculture, African Notes: Journal of the*

Institute of African Studies, Special No. 3, WORDOC, University of Ibadan, 79-82.

This paper examines the role of women in agriculture, highlighting some constraints to effective participation. In advocating the need to reduce the drudgery of women's work, it suggested the establishment of day-care centres and the provision of potable water.

16. Ijere, M.O. (1991) Promoting Women Participation in Cooperative Movement. In M.O. Ijere (ed.), *Women in Nigerian Cooperatives,* Enugu: Acena Publishers, 1-19.

This paper examines the involvement of women in the different spheres of the economy as farmers, traders and entrepreneurs. It further pointed out that the motives for women's varying roles in the economy are socio-economic, and the constraints impeding women's effective participation were highlighted. The extent women are involved in cooperatives and suggestions for their participation were discussed.

17. Ijere, M.O. (1991) The Role of Cooperatives in the Upliftment of the Lot of Nigerian Rural Women. In M.O. Ijere (ed.), *Women in Nigerian Cooperatives,* Enugu: Acena Publishers, 52-64.

This paper starts by discussing the prejudices against women that have brought about the underestimation of the role of women. It finally opined that participation of women in cooperative societies have the potential to uplift women and suggests some cooperative societies for women.

18. Ijere, M.O. (1991) An Assessment of the Better Life Programme: A Cooperative Approach. In M.O. Ijere (ed.), *Women in Nigerian Cooperatives,* Enugu: Acena Publishers, 116-135.

This paper is organised according to the following sub-headings: positive performance; essence of cooperatives; assessment of the Better Life Programme highlighting the constraints; strenghts and opportunities; solutions; and role of educational institutions to improve performance of the Better Life Programme.

19. Ijere, M.O. (1991) Women in Small-scale Cooperative Industries: Relief to Urban Migration. In M.O. Ijere (ed.), *Women in Nigerian Cooperatives,* Enugu: Acena Publishers, 20-36.

The author discusses how women in small-scale industrial cooperatives can bring about solutions to the desertion of the villages by able-bodied men and women for the urban towns. The three ways in which women can make useful contributions towards reducing rural exodus are by playing leadership roles in cooperative movement; greater decision making and participation in the cooperative; and employment in small-scale industries.

20. Iyoha, Helen (1991) Role of Women Cooperatives in Food Production. In M.O. Ijere (ed.), *Women in Nigerian Cooperatives,* Enugu: Acena Publishers, 78-91.

The author gave a brief history of modern cooperative movement, discussed the role of women in farming, processing, preservation and storage. Finally, the women cooperative societies in some states were discussed and recommendations made for improvement.

21. Jackson, Cecile (1985) The Kano River Irrigation Project. *Women's Roles and Gender Differences in Development.* West Hardford: Kumarin Press.

This study was conducted between 1976 and 1978. It consisted of a pilot survey, successive rounds of questionnaire surveys, the collection of data by less formal techniques from three nucleated settlements, and one dispersed settlement in on- and off-project situations. The focus was on the effect of the project on women and vice versa. It was found that the project did not explicitly address the needs of women, nor did it include activities expressly for them. Nonetheless, the project interventions had a direct effect on the lives and livelihood of the women in the area. Furthermore, the project affected the lives of two very different groups in the area: pagan and Moslem. The different cultural backgrounds of these women led to very different impacts and adaptations.

22. Janelid, I. (1975) *The Role of Women in Nigerian Agriculture.* Monograph based on a paper presented at the National Seminar on Home Economics Development Planning, Ibadan, 1-6 December. Rome: FAO.

This paper considers some social, religious, political, and other factors that have a negative effect on the contributions of women in agriculture. Factors such as access to land, traditional norms, exclusion of women in decision-making, lack of skills and training are highlighted.

23. Ladipo, P. (1981) Developing Women's Cooperatives: An Experiment in Rural Nigeria. In N. Nelson (ed.), *African Women in the Development Process.* London: Frank Cass & Co. Ltd., 123-136.

24. Large, O.G. (1988) The Role of Women in Food Production, Processing and Preservation in Nigeria. In T.O. Adekanye (ed.), *Women in Agriculture, African Notes: Journal of the Institute of African Studies,* Special No. 3, WORDOC, University of Ibadan, 27-35.

This paper identifies the roles of women not only in food production, but in processing and preservation, illustrating with animal and fish products. The women perform their roles using traditional agricultural technology. To enhance women's production, the paper suggests improved technology, education of women, access to credit/loans, and formation of cooperative societies.

25. Martins, S. (1984) Gender and Innovation: Farming, Cooking and Palm Processing in the Nggu Region, Southeastern Nigeria, 1900-1930. *Journal of African History,* 25(4), 411-427.

26. Nwoko, S.G. (1991) Comparative Occupational Analysis of Women in Two Selected Ibo Communities and the Effects of Food Production in Nigeria. In M.O. Ijere (ed.) *Women in Nigerian Economy.* Enugu: Acena Publishers, 106-112.

This paper is an empirical study that shows the extent of full-time farming in selected communities. The findings show that there is an increasing rate of part-time farmers among women, the implications of which is that more opportunities and specialisations should be provided to fully occupy the women.

27. Ogbonna, K. I. (1989) Factors Affecting the Productivity of Rural Women in Agriculture in Imo State. *Unpublished M.Sc. Thesis.* Department of Agricultural Extention, University of Nigeria, Nsukka, Nigeria.

This study examines the state of food production in Imo State through the identification of factors affecting the productivity of rural women as well as the extent the factors enhance or constrain their productivity. Full-time farmers were mostly illiterate and they perform over sixty percent of tasks associated with agricultural production. A majority of the women lack basic agricultural knowledge and skill and have never participated in any agricultural extension/rural development programme. Constraints to high productivity include lack of adequate labour and finance, incidence of pests and diseases, and level of education attained.

28. Okafor, R.C. (1991) The Role of Women in Cooperatives. In M.O. Ijere (ed.) *Women in Nigerian Cooperatives,* Enugu: Acena Publishers, 37-51.

This paper discusses the object of cooperatives and the role of women in cooperative leadership. Some natural characteristics of women, which can be of vital use in cooperative leadership, are solidarity, sympathy, patience, tolerance, dynamism and availability. The organization of cooperatives for women is discussed.

29. Okafor, R.C. (1991) Mobilizing Women for Cooperative Leadership. In M.O. Ijere (ed.) *Women in Nigerian Cooperatives,* Enugu: Acena Publishers, 65-77.

This paper highlights points in mobilization of women for leadership such as education, group work, and leadership training. The two objectives of a leader are to serve members, and to make a profit. The paper further discusses the duties and qualities of a leader, disadvantages of bad leadership, and how to fight the ills of bad leadership.

30. Okonjo, K. (1979) Rural Women's Credit Systems: A Nigerian Example. *Studies in Family Planning,* 10 (11/12), 326-331.

Esusu is a traditional saving system. Two hundred women were studied and ninety-five percent of them belong to this saving system. They were predominantly illiterate. The paper reveals that eighty percent of the women used the *esusu* money to pay for children's school fees or to provide school uniforms and texts. Other uses of the *esusu* savings include petty trading, hospital bills, family food and so forth.

31. Okorji, E.C. (1991) A Comparative Study of the Role of Women in Traditional and Modern Oganisations in Nigeria. In M.O. Ijere (ed.), *Women in Nigerian Economy*. Enugu: Acena Publishers, 122-133.

The indices used in the comparison are decision-making, provision of labour, and contribution to household income. Factors that influence women's role in rural and urban communities were also analysed.

32. Okorji, E.C. (1988) Traditional Sex-related Household Roles as Determinants of Income Distribution: A Case Study of Arable Farming Communities in Anambra State, Nigeria. *Tropical Agriculture*. 65(1), 89-95.

33. Olawoye, J.E. (1988) Factors Affecting the Role of Rural Women in Agricultural Production: A Survey of Rural Women in Oyo State, Nigeria. In T.O. Adekanye (ed.), *Women in Agriculture, African Notes: Journal of the Institute of African Studies*. Special No. 3, WORDOC, University of Ibadan, 23-26.

The major objective of this paper is to determine if there is any relationship between whether rural women work on the farm or not and other characteristics such as: community of residence, age, migrant status, and the position of the woman among the husband's wives. The results reveal that the role of women in agricultural production is variable, one which may change as opportunities for alternative sources of income increase with rural development.

34.Olayide, S.O. & Bello-Osagie, V.B. (1980) Roles of Women in Nigeria Small Farming. In Olayide, S.O. et al. (eds.), *Nigerian Small Farmers*. Ibadan: CARD, 143-145.

This paper discusses the importance and contributions of women to food production. It is in a small scale due to their inaccessibility to land as a result of culture and tradition. It recommends ways and means of helping women in this important role.

35. Olayiwole, C.B. (1984) Rural Women's Participation in Agricultural

Activities: Implications for Training Extension Home Economics. *Unpublished Ph.D. Thesis*, Kansas State University, Manhattan, U.S.A.

36. Onah, B.N. (1987) Rural Women's Response to Innovations Relating to Cowpea Preservation, Processing and Consumption in Isi-Uzo Local Government Area of Enugu State. *Unpublished M.Sc. Thesis*. Department of Agricultural Extension, University of Nigeria, Nsukka, Nigeria.

The main purpose of the study is to explore the pattern of cowpea usage and the problems associated with the usage in the LGA. Results reveal that seventy-nine percent of the respondents are unaware of major innovations in cowpea usage. Major problems are mould formation on fresh cowpea, weevil attack on dry seeds, and unavailability of milling machines.

37. Onunka, M.W. (1991) Women in the Cooperative Movement. In M.O. Ijere (ed.), *Women in Nigerian Cooperatives,* Enugu: Acena Publishers, 92-115.

The focus of the paper is on women participation in cooperatives with figures showing that the number of women in cooperative societies is insignificant and discouraging. Out of 1,232 registered cooperative societies in Imo State in 1978, there were only twenty-two exclusively with women membership. The paper further discussed the following: the economic and social benefits women derive from participating in cooperative societies, and the expected future role of women in consumer shops. The author concludes by making recommendations to enhance participation of women in cooperative movements.

38. Onwubuya, E.A. (1987) The Role of Rural Women as Farmers in Selected Agricultural Communities of Anambra State. *Unpublished M.Sc. Thesis*. Department of Agricultural Extension, University of Nigeria, Nsukka, Nigeria.

This study assessed rural women's roles and contributions to farming focusing on their personal characteristics, ownership of farmland, farming status, cropping, as well as animal husbandry activities performed. Other factors investigated include their attitude towards farming, participation in agricultural extension and rural education programmes, constraints to farming, and suggestions for improving their productivity.

39. Osuala, J.D.C. (1991) Enhancing Women's Economic Potentials Through Appropriate Technology. In M.O. Ijere (ed.), *Women in Nigerian Economy.* Enugu: Acena Publishers, 70-80.

This paper discusses the different technologies spawned over time to relieve drudgery for women. The author advocates a positive attitude to women's role and the provision of appropriate modalities to maximise the efforts of women. The responsibility to spearhead this rests on women academics.

40. Spiro, H. (1985) The Ilora Farm Settlement in Nigeria. *Women's Roles and Gender Differences in Development.* West Hartford: Kumarian Press.

This study examined some of the positive and negative outcomes on the Ilora farm settlement (IFS) with particular emphasis on women. One of the findings is that the failure to integrate women's economic interests is a fundamental weakness in all the projects. The study provides added commentary and insights of potential values to planners of future scheme.

41. Uwakah, C.T. & Uwaegbute A.C. (1982) The Role and Contributions of Rural Women to Agricultural Development in Eastern Nigeria. *Education and Development,* 2(2), 447-461.

Agriculture is the main occupation of rural dwellers in this part of Nigeria. The authors catalogued the role and contributions of women to sustenance of agriculture. They highlighted some constraints and suggested ways of improvement.

42. Uzuegbunam, A.O. (1987) Women in Igbo Agriculture and Commerce: The Role of Nsukka Igbo Women. Paper presented at the 2nd annual seminar on Igbo Life and Culture, University of Nigeria, Nsukka, 1-4 December.

This paper attempts to examine the various agricultural and economic activities engaged in by Nsukka women. The traditional activities of women and the added chores as a result of education and contact with non-natives during and after the civil war are identified. The significance of women's financial contributions in the families are discussed. Finally, some considered suggestions for improvements are proffered.

2

National Development

43. Adeleke, M.R.A. (1990) Women in Industrial Development in Nigeria. *Management in Nigeria,* 26(6), Nov/Dec, 14-16.

44. Adesiyan, J.O. (1990) Women, Non-Formal Education and Rural Development in Rivers State of Nigeria. A paper presented at the International Conference on Women by the Institute of Education, University of Nigeria, Nsukka, 8-12 October.

This paper attempts to look at the Women non-formal Education programmes in the Rivers State and relate it to the rural development activities going on in the State. To be able to evaluate the roles non-formal education programmes have played in the lives of the rural women, an attempt is made to look at the concepts of adult and non-formal education and their roles in the lifelong education of men and women. It also looks at the various categories of training programmes that are organised for women in the state with a view to making them participate actively well, like their men counterparts, in the developmental efforts geared towards rural areas. The paper reviews the achievements of the various non-formal education programmes, and concludes by asserting that the non-formal education programmes for the women in the state have made many of them self-reliant, and made it easy to mobilise the women for taking active roles in community development efforts. It, however, recommends that financial assistance should be given to the graduands of these programmes to make them more productive.

45. Adeyemo, R.O. (1984) Women in Rural Areas: A Case Study of South-Western Nigeria. *Canadian Journal of African Studies*, 18(3), 563-572.

46. Adigwe, H.A. (1991) The Role of Women in Socio-Cultural Development in Nigeria. In M.O. Ijere (ed.), *Women in Nigerian Economy*. Enugu: Acena Publishers, 134-155.

This paper examines the problems facing women's role in development, such as foreign orientation and men's prejudice. It further indicates guidelines for a proper approach to the problems. It concludes by advocating a fresh definition of roles, the danger of maintaining discriminatory taboos against women, and the need for equality and cooperation between the men and women.

47. Afigbo, A.E. (1991) Women as a Factor in Development. In M.O. Ijere (ed.), *Women in Nigerian Economy.* Enugu: Acena Publishers, 41-53.

The old and new roles of women in social, economic, and political development are contrasted. The author blames part of women's problems on the general attitude that women are just reserves for physical and mental resources to be ordered about and not given their due place in development.

48. Akande, J.O. (1984) Participation of Women in Rural Development. *Rural Development and Women in Africa.* Geneva: International Labour Office, 129-136.

The investigation was carried out in Oyo, Ogun, Ondo and Bendel States. It looked at the extent women have been integrated into rural development programmes. Women have been found to suffer from lack of integration into the entire rural economy and mode of production. The investigation also reveals that lack of infrastructure, credit facilities, and restriction of available resources from women put them in a disadvantaged position in development programmes.

49. Akande J.O. (1981) Participation of Women in Rural Development (Nigeria). Paper prepared for the International Labour Office, Tripartite African Regional Seminar, Rural Development and Women, Dakar, Senegal, 15-19 June 1981.

This study focuses on the involvement of women in the development process. The constraints to women's effective participation, such as illiteracy, lack of adequate health services, transportation services, adequate technology, loans, credits, and land are discussed. In addition, the study expresses the fear that introduction of new technology and improved transportation, among others, might contribute to the undermining of women's participation in and contribution to rural development.

50. Akuezuilo, M.C. (1989) Women as the Key Factor in Rural Development: Implications for Home Economics Education. Paper presented at the Nigerian Vocational Association International Conference, University of Nigeria, Nsukka, 5-6 October.

The author examined rural areas in Nigeria and what its development entails. She further highlighted the place of women and their role in rural development. The contributions of home economics education towards the realization of rural development through women were also discussed.

51. Alele-Williams, G. (1991) The Contribution of Women to National Development: Education. In NAUW (ed.), *The Contribution of Women to National Development in Nigeria*. Lagos: Nigerian Association of University Women.

52. Amucheazi, E. (1991) The Indispensability of Nigerian Women in the Positive Transformation of Rural Areas. In M.O. Ijere (ed.) *Women in Nigerian Economy*. Enugu: Acena Publishers, 113-121.

The author argues that women are indispensable in national development and therefore should be trained and equipped to play their rightful roles. He also gives specific examples of such activities that can be mounted for women to bring about their fullest potential.

53. Anambra State Better Life Unit (1989) *Anambra State Women on the Move*. Enugu: Government House, Anambra State.

This magazine was produced to celebrate the second anniversary of the Better Life Programme (BLP). The content ranged from reports from all the local government areas to BLP products in the state. There are also write-ups on women, rural banking, rural women in traditional Nigeria, tips on diet and nutrition, computer for rural women, effects of BLP in the state, and messages from well-wishers.

54. Asogwa, U.C. (1990) *Group Training and Working with Women Groups in Africa: The Nigerian Perspective*. Enugu, Nigeria: Development Education Centre.

Based on case studies and comprehensive field experience from several years of working relationships with various women's groups, the author brought to focus the constant challenges of women, especially the less privileged and the marginalised. The author considers group training with predetermined schedules, content and objectives as an effective and result-oriented effort to the mobilization and participation of women in self and community development.

55. Asogwa, U.C. (1986) Group Training as Functional Strategies for Women's Participation in Community Development. *Unpublished M.Ed. Thesis.* Department of Education, University of Ibadan, Ibadan, Nigeria.

56. Azikiwe, U. (1991) Technological Development to Enhance the Better Life Programme (BLP) in Anambra and Enugu States. Paper presented at the 5th Annual Conference of the Technological Writers Association of Nigeria (TEWAN) at Federal College of Education (Technical), Umunze Anambra State, 4-7 November.

This study was undertaken to identify areas of BLP that need technological development for enhancement. Twenty-nine women leaders were used and data were collected using the focus group discussion (FGD) technique. Findings of the study reveal that many BLP projects are stifled due to lack of equipment, electricity, and poor transportation. The paper therefore suggests that both hard and software technologies be provided for the women to make their efforts in BLP worthwhile and meaningful.

57. Azikiwe, U. (1991) Technologies for Nigerian Rural Women's Activities and Development: Case for Appropriate Technology. Paper presented at the International Conference by the Institute of Education, University of Nigeria, Nsukka, 8-12 October.

The purpose of this paper is to identify the technologies used by rural women in the performance of their roles. The survey revealed that cooking, agriculture and food production, food processing and preservation, and transportation tasks are performed with crude and primitive tools, such as firewood, hoes, grinding stone, smoking and sun-drying, trekking and so forth. Some health problems that could arise from the use of these traditional technologies were highlighted and suggestions for improvement made.

58. Azikiwe, U. (1990) Barriers to Effective Integration of Nigerian Rural Women in Development. *WID Forum,* XXII, October. Michigan State University, East Lansing, U.S.A.

This paper focuses on barriers to effective integration of rural women in national development. It specifically examines the problems created by the invisibility of women's work, the unavailability of loans and credits, illiteracy, vocational skills, and the strength of tradition and culture. The paper suggests introducing appropriate technology in order to facilitate the integration of Nigerian rural women in national development.

59. Azikiwe, U. (1990) Appropriate Technology for National Development: A Case for Rural Women in Nigeria. *WID Forum,* XXI, October. Michigan State University, East Lansing, U.S.A.

This paper reviews technological innovations that would improve the productive efficiency of rural women in Nigeria. Constraints to the successful introduction of these technologies are discussed, with recommendations for how they may be effectively implemented. It is suggested that while rural women are actively and directly involved in Nigerian development, the limitations of available technology and education have preventive contributions to national development.

60. Azikiwe, U. (1990) Women in Agriculture and Rural Development at the Crossroads: The Way Out. *Journal of the Nigerian Vocational Association.* Vol. III, November, 48-54.

The main concern of the paper was on the constraints to effective participation of women in rural development. Some of the constraints identified are: illiteracy, inadequate health care services, lack of funds, loans and land, and technologies. Suggested strategies for improvement are: use of appropriate technologies, provision of credit/loans, extension services, access to land, education, and inclusion of women in policy-making bodies.

61. Azikiwe, U. (1990) Strategies for Enhancing the Role of Nigerian Rural Women. Implication for National Development. Paper presented at the Inauguration and 1st Annual Conference of the Nigerian Chapter of the Circle of African Women Theologians, University of Calabar, Cross River State, 2-5

October.

This paper attempts to identify some factors to seriously consider when planning NFE programmes for rural women in Nigeria. A total of 1,026 non-literate, ever-married women responded to the instrument. The results showed that the rural women would gladly participate in NFE programme classes if they are conducted in the evenings; and fee-free programmes would be preferred to fee-paying ones. Recommendations were made based on the findings.

62. Azikiwe, U. (1990) A Review of Research on Women and Development in Nigeria. In R.O. Ohuche and M. Anyanwu (eds.) *Perspective in Educational Research and National Development*. Vol. 2, 70-82.

This paper reviewed both published and unpublished works on women in Nigeria. The materials were grouped into four categories, namely, role, status, and marriage; work and employment; education; and politics and law.

63. Azikiwe, U. (In Press) Technology and Educational Development in Nigeria: The Case for Appropriate Technology and Rural Women. *Journal of Technical Education Review*. Vol. 3.

This paper discussed the importance of polytechnic education, technology, and the relationship between the two for growth and development of rural areas. The need for appropriate technology for rural women for rural development in view of their contributions to agriculture and food production, domestic chores and health were discussed. Polytechnics were called upon to rise up to the challenge of producing technologies for use by rural women.

64. Bello, Sule (1985) Problems of Theory and Practice in Women's Liberation Movements. In WIN (ed.), *Women in Nigeria Today*. London: Zed Books Ltd., 23-27.

This paper looked at the women's liberation movement worldwide by identifying three dominant tendencies. It further raised questions about the position of women and what role they are destined to play in the political-economic development of Nigeria. It concludes by advising women who are concerned with oppression to address themselves to oppressive relations. They will ally with the oppressed classes in opposition to an oppressive system, which is the basis for other injustices.

65. Better Life Programme for the Rural Women (1991) *Four Years of the Better Life Programme for the Rural Women*. Lagos: National Organising Committee of the Better Life Programme.

This book is the first comprehensive attempt to collate and review the activities, achievements, and problems of the programme. The activities of the programme in twenty-one states and Abuja were covered. The publication revealed that the social, agricultural, economic and educational lives of our rural dwellers have been positively and permanently transformed through the efforts of the BLP. Through the programme the rural women have now formed various cooperative societies, acquired new skills and techniques for self and collective improvement, increased income, and have developed attitudes and values that sustain and promote self-reliance and national development.

66. Ekejiuba, F. (1991) Women in the Context of Rural Development. In M.O. Ijere (ed.) *Women in Nigerian Economy*. Enugu: Acena Publishers, 81-105.

This paper focuses on rural women, and analyses the factors which realises and maximizes women's activities and the incentives to ensure full mobilization of women. It concludes by advocating new approaches in understanding and studying women's role in rural development.

67. Ekejiuba, F. (1990) Social Capital, Social Mobility and Changing Social Status of Igbo Women. Paper presented at the Seminar on Igbo Women in Socio-Economic Change. Better Life Programme (Imo State Wing) Owerri/Institute of African Studies, University of Nigeria, Nsukka, 3-5 April.

By examining such aspects of Igbo society as the economic structure, value and kinship systems, this paper argues that Igbo society expected, respected and provided for social mobility and status enhancement of Igbo Women. It demonstrates by analysing the results of an exploratory, non-probability sample of educated Igbo women, the degree to which women exploited the diverse sources of social capital and foci of power to break the cycle initiated by colonial and post-colonial policies, of women's exclusion from being equal partners and beneficiaries of development. Education is seen as a critical factor in economic and social activities that help to break the cycle of women's exclusion as equal partners in development.

68. Ekejiuba, F. (1987) Women in the Context of Rural Development. *Nigerian Journal of Public Administration and Local Government,* June, 95-109.

69. Ekejiuba, F. (1980) Women in the Context of Rural Development. In M.O. Ijere (ed.) *Women in Nigerian Economy.* Enugu: Acena Publishers, 81-105.

In the two articles, the author analyses factors which maximise women's activities as well as discusses the incentives needed by women to ensure their full mobilization. The paper concludes by advocating new approaches in women's role in rural development.

70. Ekejiuba, F. (1985) Contemporary Households and Major Socio-economic Transitions in Eastern Nigeria: Towards a Reconceptualization of the Household. In J. Gayer and P. Peters (eds.), *Conceptualizing the Household: Issues of Theory, Method and Application,* Cambridge: 12-16.

71. Ekejiuba, F.I. (1980) Project Answer: An Organisational Framework for Integrated Rural Development. In F.I.A. Omu, P.K. Makinwa, and A.O. Ozo (eds.), *Proceedings of the National Conference on Integrated Rural Development and Women in Development.* Vol. 1. Benin City: University of Benin, 366-392.

72. Ekpeyong, L.E. (1991) Cultural and Economic Emancipation of the Rural Women Versus Paradigm - Transition Learning: Finding a Meeting Point. Paper presented at the International Conference on Women by the Institute of Education, University of Nigeria, Nsukka, 8-12 December.

A close look at the whole concept of the Better Life Programme (BLP) for the Nigerian rural women indicates an attempt at a movement away from cultural ignorance and backwardness, abject poverty and disease, to business adventurism and socio-cultural and economic emancipation. When one critically examines the process of conducting the BLP, one comes to the position that the current externally imposed non-formal approach, while it may to some extent sharpen the rural women's sense of business venture and improve their economic well-being, appears grossly inadequate to sustain their self-emancipation which is the ultimate goal of BLP. According to this paper, the rural women's self-emancipation may best be achieved through a process of paradigm-transition learning. This is a process that occurs as a result of the emergency and ascendancy of a new set of critical awareness that stimulates or compels the restructuring of established or hypothetical constructs; a set of assumptions and processes that serve to explain a domain of objective reality. How paradigm-transition and, in turn, socio-cultural and economic emancipation of the rural women can be brought about, forms the main subject of discussion in this paper.

73. Enabulele, A.B. (1985) The Roles of Women's Associations in Nigeria's Development: Social Welfare Perspective. In WIN (ed.) *Women in Nigeria Today*. London: Zed Book Ltd., 187-194.

The purpose of this paper is to examine the role of women's association in Nigeria's national development. A background of the association is presented, as well as their structure and contributions. The contributions fall into three major areas: health, education, and social. It suggested a coming together of the various women's organisations to discuss issues and their problems as they relate to women, and thereby produce a strong united body that speaks for the betterment of womenfolk.

74. Etukudo, A.T.U. (1978) Rural and Urban Household Incomes and Expenditures in Nigeria. *Human Resources Research Bulletin,* No. 78/06, University of Lagos.

75. Ezeilo, B.N. (1990) Igbo Women and Socioeconomic Change: A Psychological Perspective. Paper presented at the Seminar on Igbo Women in Socio-Economic Change. Better Life Programme (Imo State Wing) Owerri Institute of African Studies, University of Nigeria, Nsukka, 3-5 April.

The behaviour of women due to two major psychological factors, biological and environmental (socialization), are discussed.

76. Igben, M.S. (1980) Socioeconomic Activities of Women in Some Selected Nigerian Rural Communities: Implications for Integrated Rural Development in Nigeria. In F.I.A. Omu, P.K. Makinwa, and A.O. Ozo (eds.), *Proceedings of*

the National Conference on Integrated Rural Development and Women in Development. Vol. II, Benin City: University of Benin, 950-962.

77. Ijere, M.O. (1991) Women in Development. In M.O. Ijere (ed.), *Women in Nigerian Economy.* Enugu: Acena Publishers, 1-6.

The author examines the rural sector, the constraints that have dogged the pace of women in participating fully in national development, as well as the prospects that exist to realise this.

78. Izundu, N.T.A. (1991) Gender Variation in Risk-Taking Behaviour of Nigerians: Implications for Women Participation in National Development Towards the 21st Century. Paper presented at the International Conference on Women by the Institute of Education, University of Nigeria, Nsukka, 8-12 October.

This paper identifies and describes the gender variations in risk-taking behaviour of 866 randomly selected Nigerian adolescents (460 males and 406 females). Mean scores and ANOVA statistics were used for data analysis. Results show that a significant difference exists in the mean scores of subjects at .001 probability level. Based on this finding, the researcher recommended that risk-taking behaviour of Nigeria women should be enhanced so that they can help meet the challenge of nation-building alongside their male counterparts.

79. Kisekka, M. (1981) The Role of Women in Socioeconomic Development. Indicators as Instruments of Social Analysis: The Case of Nigeria and Uganda. *Women and Development: Indicators of Their Changing Role.* Unesco, 33-47.

The purpose of this paper is to establish the value of qualitative information in understanding the status of women and planning for their comprehensive involvement in the development process. The first part of the paper briefly outlines the findings of social, economic, health, educational and occupational indicators on women's status. Major constraints to women's wider participation are inferiority complex vis-à-vis males, medical, educational and legal barriers. The focus of the paper is on Hausa women in Nigeria and Babangida women in Uganda.

80. Michelwait, D.R., Riegelman, M.A., and Sweet, C.F. (1976) *Women in Rural Development: A Survey of the Roles of Women in Ghana, Lesotho, Kenya, Nigeria, Bolivia, Paragua and Peru.* Boulder: Westview Press/Development Alternative, 224p.

This study is on existing rural projects in the seven countries. It investigated the constraints and opportunities for women in these countries' economies. It also focused on rural women's active decision-making and participation in agricultural production, and the usual source of discretionary income in rural areas. Other areas covered by the study are family care, family planning, and education of children.

81. Nelson, N. (1981) Mobilising Village Women: Some Organisational and Management Considerations. In N. Nelson (ed.), *African Women in the Development Process.* London: Frank Cass and Co. Ltd., 47-58.

82. Njoku, O.N. (1990) Women in Traditional Igbo Economy. Paper presented at the Seminar on Igbo Women in Socio-Economic Change. Better Life Programme (Imo State Wing) Owerri/Institute of African Studies, University of Nigeria, Nsukka, 3-5 April.

The focus of this paper is on the traditional Igbo economy practised before it was penetrated and mediated by western presence and colonialism. The three components of Igbo economy, namely, agriculture, non-agricultural production and trade, are considered. The paper concludes that women played a vital role in all the sectors of traditional Igbo economy, and continue to do so to the present.

83. Nwafor, M.O. (1990) The Role of Women Education in Rural Development. In R.O. Ohuche and M. Anyanwu (eds.), *Perspectives in Educational Research and National Development.* Vol. 2.

84. Odu, D.B. (1989) Rural Development and Women in Occupations. Paper presented at the International Conference of the Nigerian Vocational Association, University of Nigeria, Nsukka, 5-6 October.

This paper focuses on the factors that hinder rural development and reemphasized that there cannot be any meaningful development without the participation of women. It suggests that women in various occupations should be ready to work in rural areas as change agents.

85. Ogbonna, K.I. (1989) Factors Affecting the Productivity of Rural Women in Imo State. *Unpublished M.Sc. Thesis*. Department of Economics, University of Nigeria, Nsukka.

86. Ogbudimkpa, R.N. (1986) Constraints in Nigerian Women Labour Force Participation in Development: A Male Perspective. In F.I.A. Omu; P.K. Makinwa & A.O. Ozo (eds.), *Proceedings of the National Conference on Rural Development and Women in Development*. Vol. II, Benin City: University of Benin.

87. Ogungbile, A.O. (1991) Women's Participation in Agricultural Production in Northern Nigeria. In M.O. Ijere (ed.), *Women in Nigerian Economy*. Enugu: Acena Publishers, 54-69.

The different roles of women in rural development and the factors responsible for the changes are analysed. Moreover, the involvement of women in agriculture, their problems and solutions, are examined with empirical data.

88. Okojie, C.E.E. (1985) A Basic Needs Approach to the Integration of Nigerian Women in National Development. Paper presented at a Seminar on Nigerian Women and National Development, University of Ibadan, June.

This paper emphasizes the need to integrate women into development programmes in view of the numerous roles they play in the society. It preferred a positive approach for effective integration.

89. Okoli, P.I. (1989) Rural Development and Women in Occupations. Paper presented at the International Conference of the Nigerian Vocational Association, University of Nigeria, Nsukka, 5-6 October.

This paper highlights the laudable efforts of women in rural development and suggests they should be expanded, improved, and sustained. The paper also suggested that discrimination and marginalization of women in any shape or form should be stopped. Ways and means of improving the work of the women are also suggested, such as introduction of appropriate technologies.

90. Okonjo, K. (1991) Acknowledging the Existence of Women: Its Consequences. In M.O. Ijere (ed.), *Women in Nigerian Economy*. Enugu: Acena Publishers, 156-174.

The consequences of acknowledging the existence of women in the future of rural development in Nigeria are discussed in depth. The result will be evolving a rural development concept that is gender-neutral, making the problems affecting women in the rural areas more visible, and a better qualification of women's contribution to the national income.

91. Okonjo, K. (1991) Rural Women in Nigeria: How Do Women Count? In M.O. Ijere (ed.), *Women in Nigerian Economy*. Enugu: Acena Publishers, 184-208.

The author picks issues as the numerous "hangovers" the men and society have about women. These relate to psychological, economic, demographic, political, and educational misconceptions that must be eliminated for a healthy rural and urban development in the country.

92. Okonjo, K. (1980) The Role of Igbo Women in Rural Economy in Bendel State of Nigeria. In F.I.A. Omu; P.K. Makinwa & A.O. Ozo (eds.), *Proceedings of the National Conference on Rural Development and Women in Development*. Vol. II, Benin City: University of Benin, 1017-1034.

93. Okonjo, K. (1979) Rural Women's Credit System: A Nigerian Example. *Studies in Family Planning*, 10(11/12), 326-331.

The author examines a rotating credit system adopted by rural women to ensure the availability of money for their family's financial obligations. The study reveals how women affect and are affected by development policies, and this provides indispensable information to project designers for rural women in Nigeria.

94. Okpala, J.I.N. (1990) Igbo Women in Socio-Economic Change: A

Geographical Perspective. Paper presented at the Seminar on Igbo Women in Socio-Economic Change, Better Life Programme (Imo State Wing) Owerri/Institute of African Studies, University of Nigeria, Nsukka, 3-5 April.

The author discusses the life and activities of rural women in their locational setting with special attention to potentialities and problems. Suggestions are made on strategies for enhancing progress and development among Igbo women.

95. Okpara, E.U. (1989) Women's Perception of Their Role in National Development. Paper presented at the International Conference on Educational Research and National Development by the Institute of Education, University of Nigeria, Nsukka, 9-12 March.

This study is designed to investigate the problems facing marginally educated women in Nsukka urban and also to investigate their perceptions of the roles they can play towards national development. Suggestions were made regarding the type of activities that can be planned for them to enhance their participation in the development process.

96. Okpara, E.U. (1988) Semi-educated and Uneducated Women's Perception of Their Role in National Development. In R.O. Ohuche and M. Anyanwu (eds.), *Perspectives in Educational Research and National Development*. Vol. 2. Institute of Education/Summer Education Publishers Ltd.

The aim of this study was to find out how women view their role in the development of the nation and the constraints in their way. The findings show that the women prefer motherhood to income-generating activities for self-maintenance. Some of the constraints are lack of land, capital, and child-care facilities. The researcher recommends strong and devoted leadership for women's groups.

97. Okoye, C.U. and Ijere, M.O. (1991) Role of the Better Life Programme in National Development. In M.O. Ijere (ed.), *Women in Nigerian Economy*. Enugu: Acena Publishers, 175-183.

The authors attempt a systematic analysis of the impact-making Better Life Programme from its inception to the third year of its operation. It is the view of the authors that this is a worthwhile programme that should be continued with greater intensity in the future, particularly with the application of the co-operative approach.

98. Onwubiko, H.A. (1991) The African Woman and Development in Nigeria. Paper presented at the International Conference by the Institute of Education, University of Nigeria, Nsukka, 8-12 October.

The current state of underdevelopment in Nigeria may not be reversed without a conscious reversal of the way we treat our women in Nigeria. Women make up more than 50 percent of our population, yet this large potential reservoir for development is subjected to feudal and communal slavery through the acquisition of large numbers of women by individual men to work on their farms and boost their wealth in the name of 'marriage'. These and other forms of exploitations are presented and discussed.

99. Pittin, R. (1987) Migration of Women in Nigeria: The Hausa Case. *International Migration Review,* 18(14), 1293-1314.

100. Raza, M.R. and Famoriyo, S. (1980) Integrated Rural Development as a Framework for Women's Participation in Development. In F.I.A. Omu, P.K. Makinwa, & A.O. Ozo (eds.), *Proceedings of the National Conference on Rural Development and Women in Development.* Vol. II, Benin City: University of Benin, 933-949.

101. Simmons, E.B. (1976) Economic Research on Women in Rural Development in Northern Nigeria. OLC Paper No. 10, Overseas Liason Committee, American Council on Education, Washington, D.C., U.S.A.

102. Sudarkasa, Niara (1975) National Development Planning for the Promotion and Protection of the Family. Paper presented at the Conference on Social Research and National Development in Nigeria, University of Ibadan.

This paper criticizes African national development plans, including Nigeria's Third National Development Plan (1975-1980), for their failure to conceptualize the family as an agent in programmes for the advancement of society. The author advocates the introduction of community family councils to scrutinize the type of family organization indigenous to Africa. The types of family structure that might be best suited to indigenous modernization are discussed.

103. Uchendu, P.K. (1980) The Changing Cultural Role of Igbo Women in Nigeria: 1914-1975. *Unpublished Ph.D. Dissertation.* School of Education, Health, Nursing and Art Professions, New York University, U.S.A.

104. Yanusa, Mohammed-Bello (1985) Physical Planning for the Promotion of Women Participation in Socioeconomic Activities. Paper presented at a Seminar on Nigeria Women and National Development, University of Ibadan.

3

Education and Training

105. Abdullahi, R. (1989) Science Education for Girls: A Psychological Overview. In the Women Education Branch of the F.M.E. (ed.), Report of the National Workshop on Promoting Science, Technology and Mathematics Among Girls and Women. Ikoyi-Lagos: Federal Ministry of Education-Women Education Branch, 27-30.

This report examines the psychological reasons as to why girls are not interested in science education. Some of the reasons are stereotyping, religion, absence of role models, lack of motivation, parent/teacher expectations, and poor method of teaching science. The solution according to the paper is through change of attitude in the society.

106. Abiodun, E.A. (1984) Sexual Attitudes of Adolescents in Ondo State Secondary Schools: Implications for Counselling. *Unpublished Ph.D. Thesis.* Department of Education, University of Ife, Ile-Ife, Nigeria.

The results of the statistical analysis show that respondents did not favour the exposure of adolescents to early pregnancy, abortion, venereal disease, and illegitimate children. Fifty percent had engaged in sexual intercourse, twelve percent had been pregnant, nine percent had abortions, and eight percent had contracted venereal diseases. Factors responsible include lack of sex education and counselling services in schools. It is recommended that sex education and parenthood programmes be introduced in schools as well as sex counselling services. The faculties of education should assist in the training of required personnel.

107. Achebe, C. (1979) The Social Limitations of the Academic Women to the Pursuit of Excellence. *Nigerian Journal of Education.* 2(1), 107-111.

108. Ada, M.J. (1981) The Western Type Education of Women in Ogoja Diocese. *Unpublished PGDE Thesis.* Department of Education, University of Nigeria, Nsukka.

109. Adegbie, C.A. (1987). The Effects of Adult Literacy Education

Programme on Women Participants in Selected Centres in Oyo, Oyo State. *Unpublished M.Ed. Thesis.* Department of Education, University of Ibadan, Ibadan, Nigeria.

110. Adekoya, O. (1989) Petticoats on Board: The Surveying Experience. In the Women Education Branch of the F.M.E. (ed.) *Report of the National Workshop on Promoting Science, Technology and Mathematics Amongst Girls and Women.* Ikoyi-Lagos: Federal Ministry of Education-Women Education Branch, 31-35.

The author exposes female participation in the surveying profession. The paper requests that the country should harness all her human resources and that the Nigerian women should be prepared to make some sacrifices to be successful in their chosen profession.

111. Adeoye, T.A. (1984) Disparity in Secondary Education: Case Study of Secondary Education in Kwara State. *Unpublished M.Ed. Thesis.* Department of Education, University of Ibadan, Ibadan, Nigeria.

The purpose of the study is to enable the government to perceive more clearly the futility of discriminatory attitudes between the sexes, which consequently results to much waste of human resources. The major findings include that male enrolment was almost twice that of female. Females in all-female institutions performed better than their counterparts in mixed schools. Generally, parents have preference for male children. When it comes to educational choices, the female is not highly favoured; there is disparity in the curriculum as home economics is restricted to female schools and students, and technical subjects are restricted to male schools and students.

112. Adeyanju, F.B. (1989) Female Leadership Role and Sports Development in Nigeria. Paper presented at the Sport Psychology Association of Nigeria Conference, Lagos: National Stadium Surulere.

113. Adeyanju, F.B. (1987) Nigerian Women and Sport Participation: Stereotypical Misconceptions, Reality and Future Projection. In T.A. Adedeja, & Mshelia (eds.) *Psycho-Social Perspectives of Sports.* Enugu: Fourth Dimension Publishers Ltd.

114. Adeyanju, F.B. & Venkateswarlu, K., & Omoruan, J.C. (1989) Determinants of Sports Related Conflicts in Women. *Nigerian Educational Forum,* 12(2), 337-341.

115. Afe, J.O. (1991) Women's Education and National Development in the 21st Century: Dimensions and Future Directions. Paper presented at the International Conference on Women by the Institute of Education, University of Nigeria, Nsukka, 8-12 October.

The debate has been on whether equality or equity of education should be provided. In discussing this topic, the history of women's education in Nigeria is sketched, while the dimensions and developmental trends are identified. The problems and the various attempts at equalizing education in particular reference to women are examined. Future directions for women education in national development in the twenty-first century are advocated.

116. Aghaizu-enyenwa, J. (1981) Women's Role, Influence and Perception on Environmental Planning and Housing Design. Paper presented at the International Conference on Women by the Institute of Education, University of Nigeria, Nsukka, 8-12 October.

A number of studies have revealed that there exists a polarity of values inherent amongst the female and male environmental planners in terms of design conceptualization, form, function, and space utility. Women's uniqueness in the field of environmental studies as it affects various land uses through the dogma 'women's place is in the home' has helped to shape contemporary environmental planning of human settlements. This manifests through space intensification and mixed land uses. This paper proposes that environmental studies be included in our school curricula so as to elicit virtues of planned environment. It also calls for more research effort to ascertain the degree of contribution made by women in different facets of environmental studies.

117. Aghenta, J.A. (1989) Access by Women to Scientific Studies and Technological Training. In the Women Education Branch of the F.M.E. (ed.), *Report of the National Workshop on Promoting Science, Technology and Mathematics Among Girls and Women.* Lagos: Federal Ministry of Education - Women Education Branch, 37-40.

This study is based on the premise that there is a low participation of women in scientific studies and technological training. Its purpose is to determine the academic, cultural, and social factors responsible. Results revealed that cultural factors include socialization pattern, gender stereotyping, family type, and perceived difficulties of science occupations. Socioeconomic factors are parental education and presence of family role models in a science-based occupation. Academic factors are teachers/parental encouragement, availability of science teachers, facilities for science-based occupation, and poor performance in science subjects. Based on the findings, some recommendations were made to Unesco, government, parents, schools, and so forth.

118. Ajayi, S.L., Babalola, V.O., & Ojo, T.O. (1991) The Role of Home Economics in Better Life Programme in Nigeria: A Proposal. Paper presented at the International Conference on Women by the Institute of Education, University of Nigeria, Nsukka, 8-12 October.

The government of Nigeria has evolved many strategies to improve the quality of life of people living in the rural areas of the nation. Among these is the Better Life Programme, which was originated by Mrs. Miriam Babangida, in 1987. The programme has many objectives and the field of home economics has something to offer in achieving each of the objectives of the Better Life Programme. For example, the areas of food production, processing, utilization, storage and marketing, as well as arts and crafts can be used to achieve the first and the third aims; while community health, child care and home nursing can be used to achieve the second aim. Consequently, this paper proposes the various ways in which home economics and home economists can be used to achieve the aims of the Better Life Programme.

119. Ajiboso, T.O. (1984) Women Participation in Sports in Oyo State Colleges of Education. *Unpublished M.Ed. Thesis*. Department of Physical and Health Education, University of Ibadan, Ibadan, Nigeria.

The purpose of the study is to examine the level of participation as well as factors that affect participation in sports of women in colleges. The data reveal that parental sports participation, facilities and equipment, and level of involvement in sports in the past could affect women participation in sports. Some recommendations were made to improve the situation.

120. Akande, B.E. (1987) Rural-Urban Comparison of Female Educational Aspirations in Southern-Western Nigeria. *Comparative Education,* 23(1), 75-83.

121. Akindele, B.J. (1984) The Attitude of Women to Nutritional Values in Rural Areas. *Unpublished M.Ed. Thesis.* Department of Education, University of Ibadan, Ibadan, Nigeria.

The study investigated the attitudes of women in Akinyele village towards nutritional values and the factors determining such attitudes. The results reveal that religion, race, and age have no bearing on their attitudes to nutritional values. However, their occupation, economic status, and knowledge of nutrition affect the women's attitudes to nutritional values.

122. Akuezuilo, M.C. (1993). The Image of Vocational Technical Educator - Gender Issues in Home Economics. *Nigerian Vocational Journal: NVA.* VI. November, 147 - 151.

This study focuses on the attitude of people towards vocational technical education with particular reference to sex-stereotyped attitudes about home economics. The finding reveals that many hold a feminine image of both home economics and home economists. Positive recommendations to change this attitude are made.

123. Akujuo, D. (198) Women Education: The Nations Partner in Progress. *Education Today,* 3(1), 1-4.

124. Alhassan, A.B. (1991) Adult and Non-Formal Education for the Upliftment of African Women. Paper presented at the International Conference on Women by the Institute of Education, University of Nigeria, Nsukka, 8-12 October.

In this paper, the author argues that the typical indigenous African society regarded education as an ongoing process of life. Education breeds social change that has resulted in the African woman's active participation in social, economic, and political processes. Elaborating on the concept of adult and non-formal education, the paper examines its objective within the Nigerian context and argues that it can be integrated in agricultural, health, nutrition, youth, and employment development programmes to achieve better living conditions for

African women. A proposal is made on how to uplift the African women in all spheres of development through the medium of adult and non-formal education.

125. Alele-Williams, G. (1990) Constraints to Female Education in Nigeria: Strategies for Research. A paper presented at the Workshop on the Constraints to Women Education in Nigeria, 16-20 July.

126. Alele-Williams, G. (1989) Keynote address. In Women Education Branch of the F.M.E. (ed.), *Report of the National Workshop on Promoting Science, Technology and Mathematics Among Girls and Women In Nigeria*. Ikoyi-Lagos: Women Education Branch of the Federal Ministry of Education, 9-26.

This keynote address touched on the following: the climate of STM education in Nigeria: the role of women as nation builders and STM education; causes of low response rate among girls and women in STM education; experiences of some other countries in promoting STM education among Nigerian girls and women; suggested strategies for promoting STM education among Nigerian girls and women; the call on National Association of Women Scientists (NAWS); and recommendations.

127. Alele-Williams, G. (1985) Measure to Overcome Obstacles to Equality of Access of Female Students to Higher Education Especially in Science and Technology. Paper presented at the Unesco meeting of Experts on Participation of Women in Various Areas of Higher Education, Poland, December.

128. Amaefunah, P.O. (1989) Implications of the Dominance of Females in our Educational Institutions. Paper presented at the Third Awka Annual Education Forum by the School of Education, Anambra State College of Education, Awka, 25-27 October.

This paper reviews enrollment by sex into Secondary Schools in Anambra State from 1976 to 1986. It further discusses the reasons behind the decline in male enrollment and attention is focused on the possible implications of women taking the lead in all levels of our educational system. Some recommendations are made to avert the ugly situation.

129. Amuchie, F.A. (1983) Socialisation of College Female Students into Sport:

A Study of Childhood Influences. *Journal of Nigerian Education Research Association, 3(1), 35-41.*

130. Anise, A. (1991) Women Education and Gender Roles in Nigeria. Paper presented at the International Conference on Women by the Institute of Education, University of Nigeria, Nsukka, 8-12 October.

This paper focuses on the historical and biblical origin of women vis-à-vis their expected roles in the society and relates it to the contemporary attempt by government to advance the education of women in Nigeria. In the process, the conflicts between the traditional and culturally induced womens' roles and the current attempts to advance women education are examined and put into the perspectives of gender roles' expectations in typical Nigerian homes. Gender roles expectations are then compared with current trends in women education with emphasis on emerging and attendant sociological and cultural implications. Issues are then raised and discussed as to the required line of action for improving women education within the context of given socio-cultural artifacts.

131. Anukam, H.O. (1991) Social, Psycho-Linguistic Barriers to Functional Women Education in Africa: The Igbo Example. Paper presented at the International Conference on Women by the Institute of Education, University of Nigeria, Nsukka, 8-12 October.

Language has been found to be a very useful tool for socialization, and every culture has its own language. A powerful aspect of language is the proverb, and to the Igbos it is not just a language, it is a spoken code of conduct.

This paper examines the Igbo proverbs that prescribe some roles to women; the social and psychological implication to the educated women whose developed talents contradict the proverbial prescriptions. The intimidating role of such proverbs to the women folk is equally observed. The paper also shows how women in literature have tried to fight back and the limitations of these efforts. It concludes by suggesting what should be done by the Igbo society against the discriminatory proverbs.

132. Anusiem, A.U. (1991) Women Education, Role Perception and Functioning in a Changing Society. Paper presented at the International Conference on

Women by the Institute of Education, University of Nigeria, Nsukka, 8-12 October.

This study is an attempt to find out the influence education has on womens' perception of their roles as well as their functioning in a changing society. Questionnaire and oral interview methods were used in eliciting responses from 250 respondents, mainly students. Data collected were subjected to percentage frequency and chi-square (X^2) analysis. It was discovered that education positively affects women's perception of roles. Education helps women to better appreciate their limitations and advantages in life and hence their proper functioning in a fast changing society. The implications and recommendations were presented and discussed.

133. Anyakoha, E.U. (1990) Women in Food Production: Implications for Home Economics Practice in Developing Countries. In E. Vaines, D. Badir, & D. Kieren (eds.) *People and Practice: International Issues for Home Economists*. A Series of Booklets addressing current practices for practising Home Economists around the world. Vol. 2, No. 2.

134. Anyakoha, E.U. (1991) Women Clothing-Related Business: Challenges and Coping Skills. Paper presented at the International Conference on Women by the Institute of Education, University of Nigeria, Nsukka, 8-12 October.

Clothing occupations abound and offer individuals enormous opportunities for self-employment and self-reliance. Consequently, numerous women are presently in the clothing-related business, such as hair dressing and beauty care, dress making, weaving, textile, and dyeing. There are varied categories of women in clothing-related business. These include big/small, and trained/untrained categories. Each category can be further subdivided. The largest group of women in clothing-related business who are commonly found in all nooks and corners of the streets in urban towns can be described as the small/marginally trained group. These are often made up of young women who either dropped out of school or had no educational opportunity. They offer various valuable services to the society including the offering of apprenticeship opportunities to other women. Thus they contribute to national development. They, however, do these under constraints and require on-the-job improvement. The study, therefore, was designed to investigate into the activities of women in two clothing-related businesses, their constraints, and the possible strategies for improving their efforts. The study further identified the coping skills required by the women in the clothing-related business.

135. Asonibare, J.B. (1985) Assertive Female Training: A Counselling Strategy for Inculcating Discipline in Adolescents. *Nigerian Journal of Counselling*, 1(1), 105-112.

136. Avoseh, M.B.M., & Uwakwe, C.B.U. (1991) Women's Education in Nigeria: From Domestication to Empowerment. Paper presented at the International Conference on Women by the Institute of Education, University of Nigeria, Nsukka, 8-12 October.

Through the years Nigerian women, as in most parts of the developing world, have been victims of all forms of political, cultural, economic, educational, and social injustice. The result of this oppression, especially the denial of education to women, is that a majority of the population has been refused access to participate in the development of the country. Government, in recent years, has realised this error and is taking steps to involve women in the development of Nigeria. This paper argues that the efforts by the government through agencies, especially in the area of education, are far from being solutions to the problem. Their argument is that rapid changes in the world require new knowledge, skills, and attitudes. The education of an oppressed group, like women in Nigeria, should aim at liberation and empowerment.

137. Ayozie, B.O. (1984) Attitude of Selected Nigerian Women Towards Science and Technology. *Unpublished M.Ed. Thesis*. Department of Education, University of Nigeria, Nsukka.

138. Azikiwe, U. (1993) Economic Empowerment of Women Through the Better Life Programme. A paper presented at the Symposium organised by the Better Life Programme, Enugu State Chapter during the 1993 International Women's Day Celebration, 8th March.

This paper appraised the advantages of the Better Life Programme to rural women, and emphasized the importance of non-formal education to the upliftment of rural women.

139. Azikiwe, U. (1992) An Investigation into the Non-Formal Education Needs of Illiterate Rural Women in Anambra and Enugu State. *Unpublished Ph.D. Thesis*. Department of Education, University of Nigeria, Nsukka.

This study assessed the non-formal education needs of rural women in Anambra and Enugu States. Fifty-five education needs were identified under five subject areas, namely, basic literacy; nutrition and home management; agriculture, food production and appropriate technology; income generating activities; and primary health care. The rank order of the subjects according to importance are as follows: primary health care came first, followed by basic literacy, and the fifth is agriculture, food production and appropriate technology. In addition, the study found that location influenced rating on four areas of need. Based on the identified needs, content areas of need and curricula for the five subject areas were developed.

140. Azikiwe, U. (1991) Strategies for Planning Non-Formal Education Programmes for Nigerian Rural Women. Paper presented at the International Conference on Women by the Institute of Education, University of Nigeria, Nsukka, 8-12 October.

This paper discusses some strategies to be seriously considered to provide adequate NFE programmes for rural women. 1,026 ever-married women selected from eight communities in Nsukka urban constituted the study sample. Non-Formal Education Strategies Questionnaire (NFESQ) was used for data collection. Percentage and mean scores were applied to analyse the data, and 50 percent and 2.55 were the acceptable levels for decision making. The results reveal, among others, that evening classes will best suit the rural women, and that the mother tongue will be preferred to English as the medium of instruction.

141. Azikiwe, U. (1992) Female Participation in Science, Technology and Mathematics (STM) Education: Implications on Manpower Development. In E.U. Anyakoha & R.N. Oranu (eds.) *Vocational/Technical Education and Manpower Development*. Nsukka: Nigerian Vocational Association, 89-97.

This paper revealed that there is a low participation of females in STM at the secondary and tertiary education levels. The negative effects of this on manpower development were highlighted. It is suggested that positive attitudinal change to gender stereotyping in school texts and profession would improve the situation.

142. Azikiwe, U. (1990) A Comparative Study of Enrollment Trends by Sex in Nigerian Educational Institutions. The Case for Female Education. Paper presented at the 5th Annual Conference of the Nigerian Association for Comparative Educator (NACE), University of Nigeria, Nsukka, 11-14 July, 1990.

The enrollment rates of males and females in primary, secondary, technical, polytechnic and the university in Nigeria are compared. With the exception of primary education where female enrollment is slightly higher, enrollments of females in the other institutions under study were found to be very poor. Implications of the findings for female education are examined and recommendations made to ameliorate the ugly situation.

143. Azikiwe, U. (1988) Socio-Psychological Factors Influencing Education of Non-Literate Rural Women in Nsukka Local Government Area of Anambra State. *Unpublished M.Ed. Thesis.* Department of Education, University of Nigeria Nsukka.

This study focused on socio-psychological factors influencing education of rural women in the Nsukka local government area of Anambra state. A total of 1,026 rural women were used for the study. Socio-cultural factors such as pregnancy, child rearing, domestic chores, burials, and other meetings were found to have no influence on education of rural women in Nsukka LGA. Ten out of the twenty psychological factors were found to have no influence. Other findings are that adult education classes should be organised during the evening throughout the year; medium of instruction should be women's dialect; and the programme should be free.

144. Azikiwe, U. (In press) Sex Differences in Language Use in Nigeria: What the Studies Say. In Y.K. Yusuf and Arua O. Arua (eds.), *Women and Language in Nigeria*.

This paper reviewed studies on performances and use of language between boys and girls. Results show that it cannot be ascertained that in Nigeria girls have more of a flare for language than boys. The study covered English and French.

145. Azikiwe, U. (1992) Non-Formal Education Programme for Rural Women and Rural Development in Nigeria. In S.O. Olaitan (ed.), The Nigerian Journal of Rural and Community Development, Vol. 4, 82-90.

This paper highlighted the importance of women education, constraints to their effective participation in national development, and suggested strategies for planning interventions for them.

146. Azikiwe, U. (1993) Gender Issues in Technical Teacher Education: The Nigerian Experience. *Nigerian Vocational Journal: NVA.* VI, November, 152-162.

The need to encourage more girls and women to participate in science, technology, and mathematics (STM), as well as take up STM-related jobs, have currently been the concern of both state and federal governments and non-governmental organisations. The purpose of this study, therefore, is to determine the extent of gender stereotyping in the Federal Colleges of Education (Technical). Research evidence has been presented to indicate that, in spite of the campaigns to promote STM among girls and women, there is a disparity between male and female with regards to enrollment, graduate output, and academic staff in Federal Colleges of Education (Technical). Strategies to improve the situation, such as campaigns to change societal attitude to sex-stereotyping in occupations,have been suggested.

147. Baba, N.M. (1991) Women Education and Productivity in the Home. Paper presented at the International Conference by the Institute of Education, University of Nigeria, Nsukka, 8-12 October.

Although largely unacknowledged and unrewarded, the roles women play in the homes are as vital (if not more) as any we may assign them in the factories and offices. Their roles in production, procreation, and child-rearing are roles for which we may not find ready substitutes. It is sad to note, however, that education, instead of enhancing their functioning in the homes, pulls women away to industrial/commercial centres often with unhappy consequences for the family institution, and in the long run the society at large. This paper examines the Nigerian situation, the dimensions of this educational dysfunction as it affects women productivity in the homes, and suggests ways of restoring the dignity of women in the home as stepping stone for their total liberation.

148. Badejo, B. (1988) The Role of Federal Government of Nigeria in Women's Education: An Appraisal. Paper presented at the Annual Conference of the NAEAP, May, University of Jos.

149. Bajah S.T. & Boziomo, H. (1989) Low Participation of Girls in Science, Technology and Mathematics Education: Strategies for Redress. In the Women Education Branch of F.M.E. (ed.), *Report of the National Workshop on Promoting Science, Technology and Mathematics Among Girls and Women.* Lagos: Federal Ministry of Education-Women Education Branch, 45-55.

This paper provides statistics of low enrollment of girls in STM. Strategies for improving the situation have been suggested, such as campaign for change of attitude, creating special interest groups, and providing opportunities for girls to pursue science.

150. Bamgboye, O.O. (1983) Women in Academia: A Study of Factors Affecting the Participation and Performance of Female Lecturers/Research Fellows. *Unpublished M.Ed. Thesis.* Department of Education, University of Ibadan, Ibadan, Nigeria.

151. Beckett, P. & O'Connell, T. (1976) Education and the Situation of Women: Background and Attitudes of Christians and Muslim Female Students of a Nigerian University. *Cultures and Development*, 8(1), 243-265.

152. Braimah, K.L. (1987) Class, Gender and Life Chances: A Nigerian University Study. Comparative Education Review, 31, 570-582.

153. Caldwell, J.C. (1979) Education as a Factor of Mortality Decline: An Examination of Nigerian Data. *Population Studies,* 33(3), 395-411.

This paper argues that the women's level of education, irrespective of their exposures to medical facilities and urban living, affects the levels of child survival. Hence, this paper advocates education for women as a major influence in demographic transition. This is in view of the fact that the statistical data reveals a correlation between child mortality and parental education, type of marriage, areas of residence, socio-economic and demographic data. The sample for the investigation was a total of 8,105 women from Ibadan City and the Southwest.

154. Chineme, P.O. (1990) Strategies for the Eradication of Illiteracy Among Nigerian Women. Education Today, 3(3), 26-29.

155. Chukwu, S.A. (1991) Women Education and Gender Roles in the Home. Paper presented at the International Conference on Women by the Institute of Education, University of Nigeria, Nsukka, 8-12 October.

The need for educational investment in manpower requirement is great. But women participation in education dropped significantly during the civil war followed by a resurgence of women participation in education in the early seventies. This paper discusses the purposes, modalities, and direction of one agency's (Imo State Commission for Women) efforts in contributing to the educational development of women in Imo State.

156. Chukwuma, F.C. (1989) Toward Attainment of a Scientific and Technological Culture for National Development: A Challenge to Nigerian Women.

Women, particularly mothers, represent an untapped resource group. Specific activities that mothers can engage in to promote out-of-school science learning are presented.

157. Effiong, A.A. (1985) A Study of Factors that Affect Students Enrollment into Nurse Educators' Programme. *Unpublished M.Ed. Thesis.* Department of Education, University of Calabar, Calabar, Nigeria.

Attempts are made to find solutions to the problem of poor enrollment in the nurse educators' programme by identifying factors influencing nurses' unwillingness to enrol in such programmes in Cross River State. The following variables had a significant effect on nurses' willingness to enrol: sex, family size, interest, perception of career prospects, and incentives. Career guidance in all schools of nursing was recommended.

158. Egunjobi, L. (1984) Sex Disparities in Nigeria's Educational System. *Ife Social Sciences Review* 7 (1&2), 167-182.

This paper attempts to examine the extent of male/female disparities at the different levels of the country's educational system with a view to relating this to past and contemporary policies. The author does this by briefly reviewing the situation at the global level; presenting and analysing post independence data from Nigeria at the primary, secondary and tertiary levels; making inferences to the possible determinants of the observed pattern in the country; relating the observed situation to national policies, past and present; and summarizing the main points of the paper.

159. Ehizogie, J.I.K. (1993) Women Enrolment in Vocational/Technical Education: Implications for Junior Secondary Technology. *Nigerian Vocational Journal: NVA*, VI, November, 132-146.

This study was designed to investigate the rate of enrollment in vocational/technical education courses. Enrollment of students in two colleges of Education (Technical) and one Polytechnic was studied. It was found that there are more female students in business, agriculture, and home economics education than core technical courses. The implications of these findings to the teaching of introductory technology are discussed, and recommendations made.

160. Eke, E. (1991) The Educated Woman and the Intellectual Stimulation of Young Nigerian Children. Paper presented at the International Conference on Women by the Institute of Education, University of Nigeria, Nsukka, 8-12 October.

This paper presents three theoretical models and their experiential framework to explain the role of the educated woman in guiding children's intellectual development. Both direct and indirect influences are analysed and the risk of ignoring indirect influences highlighted. The second part of the paper examines current trends and issues that give added importance to the educated woman's role in the intellectual stimulation of children. Current teacher and student enrollment patterns, the right of the child to education, and the political influence of women are interpreted. Implications for women's activities in the home, the school and the community are also discussed.

161. Elumonye, O.O. (1985) A Study of the Level of Interest of Academic Women in Public Affair: Implications for Adult Education. *Unpublished M.Ed. Thesis*. Department of Education, University of Lagos, Lagos, Nigeria.

162. Emenyonu, P.T. (1991) Reading Preferences of Females and Cultural Expectations in Nigeria. Paper presented at the International Conference on Women by the Institute of Education, University of Nigeria, Nsukka, 8-12 October.

Recent efforts to promote women education are welcome and necessary. However, the content of that education has remained relatively stable and it is the English language and literature curriculum that is the focus of this paper. Female reading preferences in Calabar are examined in view of the cultural expectation of the local community. A definition of sex stereotyping will be presented as well as a socio-cognitive model of reading.

163. Euler-Ajayi, O. (1989) Training Women: A Reflection on the Nigerian Experience. *Education Today*, 3(1), 5-11.

164. Ezewu, E.E. (1980) A Study of Sex Differences in Academic Achievement of Secondary School Student. *The Counsellor*, No. 2, 81-88.

165. Fadonugbo, B. (1991) Women in Science, Technology and Mathematics and Development of the Society. Paper presented at the International Conference on Women by the Institute of Education, University of Nigeria, Nsukka, 8-12 October.

This paper examines the participation of females in discipline of STM with a view to highlight the importance of increasing women who pursue this discipline for the scientific and technological development of the society. The enrollment trend and performance of females in science and technology will also be considered, as well as problems and future prospects of female involvement in science, technology, and mathematics.

166. Federal Republic of Nigeria (1989) Strategies for Improving Women Access to Education and Training in Science and Technology. Presented at the 4th Regional Conference on the Integration of Women in Development on the Implementation of the Arusha Strategies for the Advancement of Women in Africa, Abuja; Nigeria, 6-10 November.

This paper examined the situation in other third world and developing countries before presenting the position of women with regards to education and training in science and technology, which was backed-up with statistical data. Factors that influence women/girls' access to education and training in science and technology were highlighted, namely, socio-cultural factors, poor and ineffective guidance and counselling services, and lower enrollment at primary and secondary school levels. Strategies to improve the situation were also presented.

167. Gbobaniyi, I. (1989) Opportunities for Women in the Women World of Computer Technology in Nigeria. In the Education Branch of F.M.E. (ed.), *Report of the National Workshop on Promoting Science, Technology and Mathematics Among Girls and Women*. Lagos, Federal Ministry of Education-Women Education Branch, 55-62.

The purpose of this paper is to draw the attention of the people to the wide application of computer technology and its efficacy in all human endeavour, as well as to identify the major career opportunities and economic prospects offered by the computer and information technologies. It relates these opportunities to the issue of job stereotypes observed that placed the womenfolk at a disadvantage. Women are called upon to develop a positive attitude and interest in computer education to avoid a repeat of what happened in STM subjects and related professions.

168. George, Mary M. (1982) An Analysis of the Impact of a Home Economics Programme on Under-privileged Women in Lagos. *Unpublished Ph.D. Thesis*. UNILAG.

This research sets out to evaluate the effect of an adult education programme in home economics on the lives of the women who benefitted from it. One hundred and fifteen women from Ajegunle, thirty-five from Olodi-Apapa, fifty from Amukoko, and thirty-seven from Maroko participated in the study. Initial information on the participants was obtained through observation, interview, and questionnaire. It was discovered that the programme was beneficial to the women as it helped them acquire home management and baby care skills. Testimonies were given by husbands and children.

169. Harbor-Peters, V.E. (1991) Teacher Gender by Student Gender Interaction in Senior Secondary Three Students Mathematics Achievement. Paper presented at the International Conference on Women by the Institute of Education, University of Nigeria, Nsukka, 8-12 October.

Poor achievement in mathematics is consistently being recorded at the WAEC/GCE & SSCE examinations. Evidence has indicated that from age 17, the average performance of males exceeds that of females in mathematics. This study was conducted to ascertain whether the interaction effect of teachers and students gender could have a significant positive influence on the students' achievement in senior secondary mathematics. The result of a two-way analysis of variance used in analysing the data is reported.

170. Ibiam, J.U. (1991) Use of Games in Primary School. Implications for Women Education. Paper presented at the International Conference on Women by the Institute of Education, University of Nigeria, Nsukka, 8-12 October.

The purpose of this study was to identify games which girls play at the primary school level, that will help them to develop educationally, socially, and psychologically, thereby making them functional members of the society. One hundred and fifty girls were observed to identify the games, their rules, and the educational values of the games. The data were analysed qualitatively. Based on the findings, some recommendations were made to improve the education of women.

171. Igbokidi, J.N. (1991) The Acceptance of Population and Family-life Education as a Prelude to Women's Development. A Case Study of Six States in Nigeria. Paper presented at the International Conference on Women by the Institute of Education, University of Nigeria, Nsukka, 8-12 October.

The main focus of this study is on the need for family life or population education for women. The study used both women and influential leaders.

Suggestions are made to inform women of population education for the future.

172. Isiugo-Abanihe, I.M. (1991) Empowering Women Through Functional Literacy Education: The Prevailing Issues. Paper presented at a Seminar Organised by the Institute for the Study of Women, Mount Saint Vincent University, Canada.

173. Ivowi, U.M.O. (1989) Promoting Physics Education Amongst Females in Nigeria. In the Women Education Branch of F.M.E. (ed.), *Report of the National Workshop on Promoting Science, Technology, and Mathematics Among Girls and Women.* Lagos: Federal Ministry of Education - Women Education Branch, 63-68.

The need to encourage females to participate more in physics education, and the role they could play in science and technology, have been stressed. Research evidence has been presented to indicate that sex has no significant contribution to achievement in physics. Low enrollment of girls in physics has been attributed to cultural factors, nature of subjects, and its utility value. Suggestions were made to minimise the problems militating against women enrollment and participation in STM.

174. Izundu, N.T.A. (1991) Access of Nigerian Women to Professional and Vocational Education. Paper presented at the International Conference on Women by the Institute of Education, University of Nigeria, Nsukka, 8-12 October.

This study addresses the following issues:

1.   The extent to which Nigerian Women have access to education in general by determining the gender discrepancy in enrollment at the various school levels.

2.   The extent to which Nigerian women have access to professional and vocational education by determining the trend in gender participation in professional courses in Tertiary Institutions in Nigeria; and also looking at their enrollment in vocational courses in technical colleges, vocational school, college of technical education, polytechnic and

monotechnics.

The findings are expected to be used in making projections as to the extent of contribution of Nigerian women to national development in the twenty-first century.

175. James, M.F. (1986) Role Conflicts in Homes of Working Class Women in the University of Lagos. *Unpublished M.Ed. Thesis.* Department of Education, University of Lagos, Lagos, Nigeria.

176. Jegede, A.O. (1986) A Survey of Problems and Participation of Women in Adult Education Programmes in Cross River State. *Unpublished M.Ed. Thesis* University of Calabar, Cross River State.

This study was designed to identify problems women encounter in participating in adult education programmes. The results revealed that timing of programmes, distance of centres, child care, laziness, old age, and interesting programmes affect participation of women in adult education programmes, while marital status had no effect. The study also found that the most motivating factors for women's participation is to know how to read and write, and home management. Subjects for the study were made up of market women, farmers, and traders.

177. Kaita, H.I. (1984) Women Education in Nigeria. In Adeniji Aderalegbe (ed.), *A Philosophy for Nigerian Education.* Ibadan: Heinemann Educational Books.

178. Knipp, M.M. (1987) Women, Western Education and Change: A Case Study of the Hausa-Fulani of Northern Nigeria. *Unpublished Ph.D. Dissertation.* Northwestern University, U.S.A.

This research was designed to assess the impact of western education on Hausa-Fulani women in Northern Nigeria. Traditionally, Hausa-Fulani women who are Muslim have their roles defined and restricted by the interpretation of Islamic doctrine. The research shows that women who have attained a high level of western education no longer fit the traditional patterns of Hausa-Fulani women; they marry late, and have some say in their choice of husbands. They are no longer secluded and they enter the modern economic sector.

179. Kolo, I.A. (1991) The Symbolic Death Syndrome in Maternal Feeling for Handicapped Children. Paper presented at the International Conference on Women by the Institute of Education, University of Nigeria, Nsukka, 8-12 October.

Symbolic death is described in the parlance of special education as the feeling by parents of handicapped children that their child is dead, or worthless at best. 'Your Handicapped Child Scale' was designed to touch the feelings of mothers of handicapped children, relations of such mothers and weaning mothers of non-handicapped children in Kano metropolis. The results from the two hypotheses tested indicated that no significant difference exists between the categorised differences judging by their feelings (as touched) about maternal needs of handicapped children.

180. Longe, J.V. (1991) Social and Psychological Foundations for the Education of African Women. Paper presented at the International Conference on Women by the Institute of Education, University of Nigeria, Nsukka, 8-12 October.

It is the concern of this paper to propose strategies on how to achieve the objectives of women associations in this regard. The paper looks at how women's education should be organised within the framework of the New National Policy on Education. It proposes a curriculum guide with suggested instructional procedure that will be appropriate for the education of the women. Other factors looked at include the human resources to be involved, provision and utilization of facilities and equipment, and how to fund the training programme.

181. Maduabum, M.A. (1991) Women Education in Science: A Sine Qua Non in Human Resource Development. Paper presented at the International Conference on Women by the Institute of Education, University of Nigeria, Nsukka, 8-12 October.

This paper addresses the issue of women education in science within the Nigerian context. It pinpoints the rationale for its advocacy and highlights the factor responsible for the persistence of gender inequality of access to education, especially higher education. The paper suggests intervention strategies to enhance equality of access to education for women-folk within the overall context of according the nation the full contribution of its citizens.

182. Maduabum, M.A. (1990) Superstitious Beliefs and Child Rearing Practices as Impediment to Effective Science Teaching in Nigeria: The Way Out. In B.C. Emenogu, O.V.N. Okoro, & M.O. Ofoefuna (eds.), *Perspectives in Teacher Effectiveness*. Onitsha: Orient Publishers (Nig) Ltd., 136-142.

183. Maduewesi, J.E. (1988) Parental Perception of Male and Female Teacher Classroom Behaviour. *International Journal of Educational Research,* Vol. 2., 67-76.

This paper determines the attitudes of some parents towards the teaching behaviour of male and female teachers. The results reveal that each sex of parents rated teachers of its gender consistently higher.

184. Makanju, O.A. (1984) Some Factors Affecting Girls Participation in Sports in Some Secondary Schools in Ibadan Municipality. *Unpublished M.Ed. Thesis.* Department of Physical and Health Education, University of Ibadan, Ibadan, Nigeria.

The findings indicate that some beliefs, attitudes, academic work, and close associates are the influencing variables resulting in low participation in sports by girls. However, socioeconomic factors, violence in sports, and material rewards do not affect girls participation in sports.

185. Mallum, J. (1990) Implication of Material Employment on Early Childhood Education. *Journal of Special Education and Rehabilitation,* 1(20), October, 80-94.

186. Masha, G.I. (1979) Occupational Preferences, Cognitive and Affective Factors in Female Students in Nigeria. *Unpublished Ph.D. Thesis.* University of Wales, United Kingdom.

187. Mbipom, G. (1983) A Study of Self-Perceived Roles of Female Administrators and Their Roles as Perceived by Teachers and School Board Members in Cross River State of Nigeria. *Unpublished M.Ed. Thesis.* Department of Education, University of Calabar, Calabar, Nigeria.

The author determines the role perception of female administrators of secondary schools in specific tasks, as well as the influence of background factors like teaching and administrative experience, grade, and setting. The paper concludes that the role perception of a female administrator is influenced more by her administrative experience and the setting of the school, than by any other factor.

188. Mgbodile, T.O. (1991) Stress Management Education: A Vital Component of Women Education for the 21st Century. Paper presented at the International Conference on Women by the Institute of Education, University of Nigeria, Nsukka, 8-12 October.

Stress management education has become a new vital element of education for the modern woman of the 21st century. The complexity of modern society, the rapid changes and demands of modern living, and the changing roles of women have all combined to trigger a new pressure wave that inevitably affects the physical, emotional, and psychological well being of the modern woman, as well as threaten the solid foundation of family life. This paper looks at women education in the context of pressures and stress conditions that have become a part of modern living.

189. Mohammed, N. (1987) Educational Opportunities for Women: What Obstacles? Paper presented at the 9th Annual Conference of the Education Studies Association held at the University of Calabar, Cross River State, 24-28 February.

The author highlights some constraints that set women back from making use of available educational opportunities. Traditional beliefs and cultural attitudes that stereotyped roles in the society, early marriage, religious practices such as *Purdah,* and economic factors are discussed.

190. Nwabuisi, E.M. (1991) The Appropriateness of Three Foreign Psychological Instruments for Measuring Test Anxiety in Nigerian Female Students. Paper presented at the International Conference on Women by the Institute of Education, University of Nigeria, Nsukka, 8-12 October.

Two test anxiety instruments and Rotter's (1966) Internal-external locus of control scale were used to measure test anxiety in Nigerian female students. The aim was to find out if these instruments were appropriate in diagnosing test anxiety in Nigerian female students. A total of 361 female and 336 male students participated in the study. Six hypotheses guided the study. The analysis of variance used to test the hypotheses showed that:

a.   There was a significant difference between the female students' self report on test anxiety 1 and test anxiety 2 measures.

b.   There was no significant difference between the female students' self report on test anxiety 1 and locus of control instruments.

c.   There was a significant difference between the female students' self report on test anxiety 2 and locus of control scales.

d.   There was no significant difference between male and female students' self reports on test anxiety 1.

e.   Their self report on test anxiety 2.

f.   Their report on locus of control.

The result of the study also showed that the mean scores of female students were consistently higher than those of their male counterparts, thus, showing that female students were more test anxious and more external in their locus of control than male students.

191. Nwachukwu, V.C. (1991) What is the Image of the Female Teacher? Ask the Children. Paper presented at the International Conference on Women by the Institute of Education, University of Nigeria, Nsukka, 8-12 October.

Drawings convey the expressive power of children. In relation to the classroom, they can be used to assess children's perception of the female teacher. This study employs such an approach. Findings are presented as a basis for understanding the proper functioning of the female teacher in the Nigerian primary school.

192. Nwachukwu, V.C. (1991) Attitudes of Women Towards Higher Education.

Paper presented at the International Conference on Women by the Institute of Education, University of Nigeria, Nsukka, 8-12 October.

Relative to the past, enrollment of women into higher education programmes is on the increase in Nigeria. What is not certain is the nature of the regard that women have for higher education. This study explores such attitudes especially in light of their implications for achievement motivation. An adaptation of Osgood's Differential Scale is used as an instrument for the study. The findings form the basis for a number of recommendations.

193. Nwafor, O.M. (1990) The Role of Women Education in Rural Development. In C.O. Ohuche & M. Anyanwu (eds.), *Perspectives in Educational Research and National Development,* Vol. 2. Onitsha: Summer Education Publishers Nig., Ltd., 200-212.

This paper argues for the education of women as an instrument for development. It examines the likely effects of rural womens' education on some attributes of rural development. The contents of programmes for the education of rural women are suggested.

194. Nwagbara, G.U. (1989) The Knowledge Gap Hypothesis: Nigerian Educated Women and Information Acquisition. *Unpublished M.A. Thesis.* Department of Mass Communication, University of Nigeria, Nsukka, 65pp.

The author examines how informed Nigerian women feel about public affairs issues. The results reveal that a knowledge gap exists between women and the information available. The number of women who are informed is not encouraging. Education, interest, age, and marital status do not have any effect on womens' level of information acquisition. It is therefore assumed that the factor responsible is gender.

195. Nwankwo, J.M. (1991) Women Education, Family Size and National Development. Paper presented at the International Conference on Women by the Institute of Education, University of Nigeria, Nsukka, 8-12 October.

This paper integrates research literature on gender discrimination, family decision making, family planning, family size, and women status. It discusses the improvement of women status through education, and the contribution of women in the overall development of the nation. The paper advocates that care, concern, and seriousness should be given to women education so that their role performance would be enhanced and reflected in the society in terms of population control, nutritional status, health, and the total network of the nation.

196. Nzewi, U.S. (1991) Factors Related to Low Female Participation in the Sciences. Paper presented at the International Conference on Women by the Institute of Education, University of Nigeria, Nsukka, 8-12 October.

It has been observed that few females participate in the sciences in Nigerian secondary and tertiary institutions when compared with the population of the boys. Since females are an important force, it has been suggested that their minor participation can lower the degree of development and advancement of science and technology in the country. This study therefore investigated the factors related to low female participation in the sciences in Nigeria. Some of the factors identified were school factors, social factors, the nature of science, occupational aspirations, and teachers influence. Suggestions were made on how to turn the identified factors into positive use in increasing female participation in the sciences.

197. Obasi, M.N. (1986) Education and the Changing Role of the Nigerian Women: A Case Study of the Imo State Women. Unpublished M.Ed. Thesis. Department of Education, University of Port Harcourt, Rivers State, Nigeria.

198. Obasi, V.A. (1991) Women Education and Gender in the Home. Paper presented at the International Conference on Women by the Institute of Education, University of Nigeria, Nsukka, 8-12 October.

The African woman has been willing to respond to economic opportunities, but has been constrained in a number of ways by problems related to the general level of economic development. This has imposed a heavier burden of housework and child rearing. In effect, this paper intends to discuss the socio-biological and historical contexts affecting the education of women; the working women in the town; gender roles; relationship between education and development and so on.

199. Obayan, A.O.I. (1991) Womens' Access to Education and Changing Gender Roles: Implications for Counselling and Development in the 21st Century. Paper presented at the International Conference on Women by the Institute of Education, University of Nigeria, Nsukka, 8-12 October.

Education is a fundamental and basic human right, and as such, women should not be left out. Women's access to education has taken up varying dimensions. National policies concerning this have also been changing over time. It is the main concern of this paper to examine womens' access to education in relation to gender roles in the home and in the society at large. Various perspectives are examined. Changing trends in sexism in relation to the proposition of an endogenous standard are also examined. Implications for counselling and national development for the 21st century and recommendations based on these are addressed.

200. Obemeata, J. (1983) Development and Implementation of a Curriculum for Nigerian Nurses. *Journal of Nigerian Education Research Association,* 3(2), 51-62.

201. Obi, C. (1993) Business Education Students' Perception of Women Managers. *Nigerian Vocational Journal:* NVA, VI, November, 61-68.

The study surveyed 180 business education students regarding their perceptions of women in management. The investigation focused on male and female students' acceptance of women managers, the extent to which students perceived women managers as being accepted by others, and a comparison of descriptions of a typical female manager. Findings conclude that business education students would prefer a male boss to a female.

202. Obioma, G.O. & Ohuche, R.O. (1980) Sex and Environment as Factors in Secondary Schools Mathematics Achievement. ABACUS, 15(2).

203. Odeyemi, O.O. (1987) Steering Girls Towards Science Technology and Mathematics. An invited lecture delivered at the Zonal Activities on Women Education Campaign, Ondo State under the auspices of the Federal Ministry of Education, Lagos.

204. Odokara, E.O. (1976) A Study of the Relevancy of the Entry Motivations of Women Adult Literacy Teachers and the Effectiveness of Teachers After Teaching. *Adult Education in Nigerian,* 1(2), 58-65.

205. Odokara, E.O. (1975) Programmes of Adult Education for Women. Action Research Series, No. 12.

This paper focuses on some programmes for educating adult women in Nigeria. The discussion was under the following headings: level of literacy needed by women to enable them to play their roles effectively; the obstacles in organising literacy programmes for women, and how to overcome them; the content of literacy education for women; and the best organisations to be responsible for the programmes.

206. Odu, D.B. (1991) Education and Self Fulfilment of Women. Paper presented at the International Conference on Women by the Institute Education, University of Nigeria, Nsukka, 8-12 October.

One of the most important goals of women education is that of strengthening society's view of what women can achieve and rebuilding women's self-image and self-confidence so that they are not under utilized. This two-fold goal has to be properly incorporated into the objectives of both the pedagogical and andragogical education of women. Women educators, and those who have the interests of women at heart, should find ways to identify every woman as a unique person who needs self-fulfilment and to properly place her alongside her male counterpart in ways that will not inhibit or destroy her individuality. Suggestions are given for educational programmes that can provide educational experiences that can lead to self-fulfilment.

207. Odu, D.B. (1986) Changing Cultural Concepts in Women's Lives in Nigeria: Implications for Educators and Counsellors. In T. Ipaye (ed.), *Educational and Vocational Guidance: Concepts and Approaches.* Ife: University of Ife Press.

208. Odu, D.B. (1983) The Needs and Challenges of Vocational Education for the Rural Nigerian Women. *Ilorin Journal of Education,* Vol. 3., February, 47-57.

209. Odumosu, M.O. (1982) The Response of Mothers to Health Education and the Incidence of Gastroenteritis Among Their Babies in Ile-Ife, Nigeria. *Social Science and Medicine,* 16(14), 1353-1360.

This paper evaluates the behavioural response to methods of hygiene taught to nursing mothers about their babies' feeding utensils by health workers, as well as investigates the incidence of gastroenteritis among babies who attend the clinic. In the analysis, consideration was given to the environmental conditions under which respondents lived. The response of the mothers was positive to health education. There was a significant difference in the incidence of diarrhoea among babies at the one percent level whose mothers were exposed to health education.

210. Offorma, G.C. (1991) Female Students' Stress: A Case Study of the University of Nigeria, Nsukka. Paper presented at the International Conference on Women by the Institute of Education, University of Nigeria, Nsukka, 8-12 October.

The purpose of this study is to identify some stress areas encountered by the female students during the sandwich programme and to make recommendations for the improvement of the situation. A stress questionnaire was administered to 1,000 female students to identify the stress areas. The variables studied include age, family size, family age, level of education, and environment. The data collected were analysed using mean scores and t-test to answer the posed research questions and formulated hypotheses. Based on the findings, some recommendations are made for a stress-free academic environment so that the aims of the programme will be achieved.

211. Offorma, G.C. (1991) Female Enrollment Pattern in the Primary School in Nigeria: Implications for Women Education. Paper presented at the International Conference by the Institute of Education, University of Nigeria, Nsukka, 8-12 October.

The purpose of this study is to identify the enrollment pattern of girls in primary schools in Nigeria. Data are collected from reports rendered by State Ministries of Education to the meeting of Joint Consultative Reference Committee on Education. It was identified that the percentage of girls who enrolled in primary school was lower than that of boys and that the proportion is still lower in the northern states than in the southern states of Nigeria. The implications of these findings were discussed and recommendation made for enhancement of women education.

212. Ogunlade, (1991) Enrollment of Women in the Sciences in Tertiary Education: A Case Study of Adeyemi College of Education. Paper presented at the International Conference on Women by the Institute of Education, University of Nigeria, Nsukka, 8-12 October.

This study set out to examine the enrollment pattern of women in the sciences in tertiary education to identify the problems responsible for low women enrollment. Adeyemi College of Education was used as a case study. The results indicated that low enrollment of women in sciences in tertiary education has its genesis in girls' poor science background, lack of interest in Mathematics in GCE O/L or WASC, defective science teaching in schools, derogatory attitudes of girls to sciences, and thin or skeletal career guidance and counselling services. Further results indicated a rather low enrollment in science - mathematics by female teacher trainees. The implications of these and other findings are presented and discussed in this paper.

213. Ogunta, G.O. (1989) Work Experiences of Females in Science-based Occupations in Imo and Rivers States of Nigeria. *Unpublished M.Ed. Thesis.* Department of Education, University of Nigeria, Nsukka.

214. Okafor, L.C. (1989) Comparative Study of the Administrative Performance of Male and Female Principals as Perceived by Teachers. *Unpublished M.Ed. Thesis.* Department of Education, University of Nigeria, Nsukka.

215. Okedara, C.A. (1976) Non-Formal Education and the States of Nigerian Women. Paper presented to the National Conference on Nigerian Women and Development in Relation to Changing Family Structure held at University of Ibadan, Nigeria, 26-30 April.

The state of art of participation of women in NFE in Nigeria was presented. The participation of women as opposed to men was found to be very poor. However, bearing in mind the population of women, the author feels an increase in the number of women between 1960 and 1970 is insignificant. The advantages of educating women were highlighted and hence the author recommends that the governments and voluntary organisations should join hands to educate women through public enlightenment, adult literacy classes, and non-formal education programmes for acquisition of skills and knowledge.

216. Okeke, E.A.C. (1990) Gender, Science and Technology in Africa: A Challenge to Education. Paper presented at the Annual Rama Mehta Public Lecture, Radcliffe College, Harvard University, Cambridge, U.S.A., February 8.

217. Okeke, E.A.C. (1990) The Role of Educational Research in Enhancing the Participating of Women in National Development. In R.O. Ohuche and M. Anyanwu (eds.), *Perspective in Educational Research and National Development*. Vol. 2. Onitsha: Summer Educational Publishers (Nig.) Ltd., 223-240.

This paper is written against the background of increasing concern to involve women in national development. It presents the state of research on women education in Nigeria in comparison with what is obtainable in other countries.

218. Okeke E.A.C. (1989) Promoting Science, Technology and Mathematics (STM) Education Among Girls and Women: Review of Initiatives. In the Women Education Branch of F.M.E. (ed.), *Report of the National Workshop on Promoting Science, Technology, and Mathematics Among Girls and Women*. Lagos: Federal Ministry of Education/Women Education Branch, 69-78.

This paper attempts to provide insight into the state of affairs and intervention programmes currently being used in other countries to encourage girls to study STM. Nigeria is advised to opt for some of the interventions or to formulate suitable intervention programmes.

219. Okeke, E.A.C. (1988) Women in Technology in Nigeria. In Farugui, A.M., Hassan, M.H.A., & Sandri, G. (eds.), *Proceedings of the Conference on the Role of Women in the Development of Science and Technology in the Third World*. ICTP Trieste.

220. Okeke, E.A.C. (1987) Attracting Women to Science Based Occupations: Nigerian Experience. *Gender Stereotyping in Science, Technology and Mathematics Education*. Report of the Commonwealth Africa Regional Workshop, Accra: Ghana.

221. Okeke, E.A.C. (1980) The Role of Women in Science Education. In E.I. Alonge (ed.), Proceedings of the Inaugural Conference of all Africa Association of Science Teachers. University of Lagos, 25-30 August, 260-269.

222. Okeke, E.A.C. & Nnaka, C. (1989) Sex Factor in Science Achievement Oriented Researches: A Review.   Paper presented at the International Conference on Educational Research and National Development by the Institute of Education, University of Nigeria, Nsukka, 9-12 March.

This paper collects the findings and explanations regarding the achievement of women in science.Selected research works in this area are reviewed and critically analysed. Recommendations were made.

223. Okeke, E.A.C. & Oreh, C.I. (1992) Women as Agents of Peace/Peace Education and African Survival. Paper presented at the International Conference on Peace Education, University of Nigeria, Nsukka, 6-9 May.

Since women lay the foundation of peace in their homes, this paper advocates the involvement of women in the peace negotiation process.

224. Okeke, E.C., Nweke, F.I., & Nnanyelugo, D.O. (1988) The Consequences of Absence of Adult Males on the Nutritional Status of Members of Rural Farm Households and Implications for Rural Development Programmes: A Case Study. In T.O. Adekanye (ed.), *Women in Agriculture, African Notes: Journal of the Institute of African Studies*. Special No. 3, WORDOC, University of Ibadan, 69-76.

This paper examines the impact of the absence of adult males on the nutritional status of rural families. The research concludes that the nutritional status of the family is lower than that of households which have male adults.

225. Okeke, R.J. (1991) Women and Special Education: The Role and Problems

Women Encounter with Handicap Children in the Family. Paper presented at the International Conference on Women by the Institute of Education, University of Nigeria, Nsukka, 8-12 October.

The primary focus of this paper was on the role and kinds of problems that Nigerian mothers encounter in their attempts to integrate a severely mentally retarded child with cerebralpalsy (spasticity) into the family. The author discussed the mother's roles and social-emotional and interpersonal problems, and considered some of the ways in which professionals might be helpful to mothers in dealing with these problems. The use of group discussions, task analysis method, as well as individual and family therapy were described as modalities for handling some of the issues that arise in coping with a handicapped child.

226. Okojie, C.E.E. (1989) Improving the Quality of Life for Rural Women in Nigeria: The Role of Education and Technology. In Uzo Igbozurike and Raza (eds.), *Rural Nigeria, Development and Quality of Life*. ARMTI Seminar Series, No. 3.

227. Okoye, N.N. (1982) Are Boys Better Than Girls in Mathematics and English? *The Counsellor,* No. 3, 121-129.

228. Okpara, E.U. (1991) Inculcation of Permanent Literacy for National Development: Implications for Mothers. Paper presented at the International Conference on Women by the Institute of Education, University of Nigeria, Nsukka, 8-12 October.

It has long been established through the works of researchers and other experts that education is the most effective tool for national development. It is also known that the home plays an invaluable role in the education of the child. Emphasizing the importance of learning, psychologists taught us that man's survival, the versatility of his adaptation to diverse environments, and the joys of abstraction in arts and science are founded on his capacity to learn.

A survey of relevant literature reveals that without language, learning cannot take place. Using teachers, some of whom are parents, the writer tried empirically to identify the ways and means through which mothers in a developing nation can assist in laying the foundation for and also improving the verbal aptitude among their pre-school and school-age children in order to facilitate learning. Recommendations are offered to mothers and women in general.

229. Oluwole, Y.A. (1989) Agricultural Education for Women in Nigeria.In the Women Education Branch of F.M.E. (ed.), *Report of the National Workshop on Promoting Science, Technology, and Mathematics Among Girls and Women.* Lagos: Federal Ministry of Education/Women Education Branch, 79-88.

The objective of this paper is to show that women have contributed tremendously to agriculture and the food system in Africa, albeit at the subsistence level. These contributions have been made under very difficult social, political, economical, and educational situations, which need to be alleviated if the potentials of women are to be fully realised. The paper is of the opinion that the female role in the system will continue to be seen as inferior to the male counterpart unless its quality is improved through modern science and technology.

230. Oni, G.A. (1985) The Effects of Women's Education on Post-partum Nonsusceptible Period in Ilorin, An Urban Community in Nigeria. *Unpublished Ph.D. Dissertation.* John's Hopkins University, Ann Arbor, Michigan.

231. Onibokum, O.M. (1979) Sex Differences in Quantitative and the Attitude Cures. ABACUS 14(1), 52-58.

232. Onuwa, G.M.C. (1991) Women Education: The Implications for Marriage Chances and Gender Roles in the Igbo Ethnic Group of Nigeria.Paper presented at the International Conference on Women by the Institute of Education, University of Nigeria, Nsukka, 8-12 October.

The belief in the biological and genetic roles of women seems to cut across cultures. These roles also seem to have been altered by the rate at which the women folk acquire higher education in recent times. This alteration engineered by acquisition of higher education seems to have some serious implications for the chances of unmarried educated young ladies. This paper critically examines the implications of acquisition of higher education in the Igbo ethnic group on:

1.   marriage chances of the unmarried educated women
2.   gender roles and marriage stability.

233. Onwubiko, G.N. (1991) Women and the Dissemination of Scientific Culture in Nigeria. Paper presented at the International Conference on Women by the Institute of Education, University of Nigeria, Nsukka, 8-12 October.

The present state of poverty and underdevelopment in Nigeria, in part , results from the absence of a scientific culture in our society. The level of scientific culture in any society is directly dependent on the level of scientific and qualitative education of the women of that society. Because women spend more time training children than any other human social group, encouraging women to acquire scientific knowledge will probably enhance the rate of the dissemination of scientific culture among our children.

234. Onwuka, U. (1990) Igbo Women in Education. Paper presented at the Seminar on Igbo Women in Socio-Economic Change. Better Live Programme (Imo State Wing) Owerri/Institute of African Studies, University of Nigeria, Nsukka, 3-5 April.

This paper starts with a brief historical account of educational opportunities for women and the need for women education. It goes on to examine what part Igbo women have collectively played in education in Nigeria and how the education they received has placed them vis-à-vis the task of the development of Igbo land in particular and of the country in general. Suggestions to make education more meaningful to women in society are made.

235. Orekie, E.N. (1984) An Assessment of Selected Education Programmes for Female Attendants of Health Centre in Lagos State. *Unpublished M.Ed. Thesis.* Department of Education, University of Lagos, Nigeria.

236. Osafehinti, I.O. (1988) Sex-Related Difference in Mathematics at the Secondary School Level. ABACUS, 18(1), 80-87.

237. Osibodu, B.M. (1989) Improving the Access of Girls and Women to Mathematics and Mathematics-Related Education. In the Women Education Branch of F.M.E. (ed.), *Report of the National Workshop on Promoting*

Science, Technology, and Mathematics Among Girls and Women. Lagos: Federal Ministry of Education/Women Education Branch, 89-94.

This paper attempts to identify some of the problems associated with low participation of girls in STM, especially in mathematics. It further examines some of the strategies employed worldwide to redress the situation and finally advances some suggestions for improving the access of girls and women to STM in Nigeria. Issues such as removing sex stereotyping in STM textbooks, segregation of girls and boys into single sex groupings for mathematics, and so forth are discussed.

238. Osibudu, B.M. (1985) Technology Education and Girl's Participation in Nigeria. Proceedings of GASAT 3 Conference. London: Chelsea College, University of London.

239. Osinkalu, Y.O.K. (1989) Identification of Problems Associated with Low Participation of Girls in Science, Technology and Mathematics (STM). In the Women Education Branch of F.M.E. (ed.), *Report of the National Workshop on Promoting Science, Technology, and Mathematics Among Girls and Women.* Lagos: Federal Ministry of Education/Women Education Branch, 95-104.

This paper identified the following as problems: tradition, culture and religion, social influence, sexism in the curriculum, teachers, and the concept of inequality. It further suggested steps to promote STM among girls and women, such as education of parents to encourage and invest in their daughters, counselling for girls, and programmes to popularise STM for girls and women.

240. Osinowo, O.O. (1984) Participation of Women in Adult Education Classes in Ogun State, Nigeria. Department of Education, University of Ibadan, Ibadan, Nigeria. *Unpublished M.Ed. Thesis.* Department of Adult Education, University of Ibadan, Ibadan, Nigeria.

This study identified social and educational factors that affect participation and motivation in programmes. Results indicate that women will participate regardless of the nature of the courses, husband's dispositions, age or marital status. Factors responsible for poor participation and performance include proximity to centre, time, family size, and responsibilities.

241. Omotola, B.D., & Akinyele, I.O. (1985) Infant Feeding Practices of Urban Low Income Group in Ibadan. *Journal of Home Economics*, Vol. 1, June, 105-116.

This study used 915 infants as its subjects and the questionnaire as the instrument for data collection. The results reveal that all the children were breastfed for varying periods starting from birth. About 80 percent were breastfed within 48 hours of delivery. Most mothers claimed to have discarded the colostrum produced in the first 24 hour post-partum. Culture played no significant role in infant feeding practices.

242. Osuala, J.D.C. (1991) Empowerment of Nigerian Women Through Adult Basic Education. Paper presented at the International Conference on Women by the Institute of Education, University of Nigeria, Nsukka, 8-12 October.

This article examines the nexus between Nigerian women's struggle for role fulfilment and adult based education. The women in the study experienced staggering disparities between their illiteracy and their optimal role expectations. As middle-aged workers and mothers of large families, they undertook a self-initiated study in adult evening classes. Through the modality of the Focus Group Discussion (FGD) method , the women revealed their role-related problems and the specific ways by which adult basic education had empowered them to be self-actualizing in their traditional roles.

243. Osuala, E.C. & Osuala, J.D.C. (1986) Occupational Satisfaction of Women Business Education Teachers and Their Husbands in Eastern States of Nigeria. *Journal of Technical Teacher Education*, Vol. 1, 40-52.

244. Saad, G. (1991) Women Education and Gender Roles in Hausa Society. Paper presented at the International Conference on Women by the Institute of Education, University of Nigeria, Nsukka, 8-12 October.

Roles are socially assigned to different sexes in every society. These roles to a large extent govern the behaviour and aspirations of individuals. Similarly, the society views whatever one does or tries to do in the context of its approved role for him or her. This paper examines the gender roles in Hausa society and their implication for the education of women.

Hausa society is one of the societies in Africa where women education is faced with a lot of hurdles, most of them rooted in the roles expected of them by the society, especially the home-based roles. This situation has a lot of implications for the education of Hausa women and is to a large extent responsible for the present low number of educated Hausa women.

245. Tibenderana, P.K. (1985) The Beginnings of Girls' Education in the Native Administration Schools in Northern Nigeria, 1930-1945. *The Journal of African History,* 26(1), 93-95.

246. Uba, A. (1985) Counselling Female Students Among Two Nigerian Ethnic Groups. *Nigerian Journal of Counselling,* 1(1), 9-14.

247. Ubogu, R.O. (1986) A Study of Mother's Education, Childcare Practices, and Infant/Child Survival in Lagos Metropolitan Area. *Unpublished M.Ed. Thesis.* Department of Education, University of Lagos, Lagos, Nigeria.

248. Udeani, U.N., & Achebe, N.E. (1991) Characteristics, Productivity and Professional Contributions of Female Nigerian Academics: A Case Study of the University of Nigeria, Nsukka. Paper presented at the International Conference on Women by the Institute of Education, University of Nigeria, Nsukka, 8-12 October.

This study assesses the employment characteristics, relative productivity, professional recognition, and professional identification of the Nigerian female academic who is primarily employed full-time in the University of Nigeria. All female academics in the fourteen faculties of the university were selected for the study. Using a 25-item structured questionnaire for data collection, the following are some of the major findings: Female academics prefer some academic disciplines to others; 71 percent of the subjects are in the junior academic cadre, few in the intermediate and very few in the professional cadre; and 88 percent of the subjects have at least two published articles. In the area of book publishing, there are very few authors. Only 10 percent of the subjects have been honoured with a professional fellowship.

249. Ugwuegbu, Denis Chimaeze E. (1978) Education Orientation and the Nigerian Students Attitudes to Husband/Wife Relations. *The Journal of Social*

Psychology, 106, 121-122.

This study was conducted among a sample of 170 female and male University of Ibadan undergraduates of Ibo, Hausa, and Yoruba descent, who were majoring in education and the social sciences. Females from Hausa evidenced traditional bias against Western education for women; they expressed the view that women with eight years formal education would not be good home-makers. They expressed more negative attitudes towards equality of educational opportunity for both sexes.

250. Ukegbu, N.N. (1980) An Investigation of the Reading Interests of Housewives and Their Use of the State Central Library in Enugu. *Unpublished MLS Thesis.* Department of Library Science, University of Ibadan, Ibadan.

251. Umoh, S. (1985) Study of the Attitudes of Nigerian Adolescents from Literate and Illiterate Homes Towards Women Participation in Higher Education. *Nigerian Journal of Counselling,* 1(1), 97-104.

252. Uwaegbute, A.C. (1987) Infant Feeding Patterns and Comparative Assessment of Formulation Weaning Food Based on Vegetable Proteins. *Unpublished Ph.D. Dissertation.* Department of Home Science and Nutrition. University of Nigeria, Nsukka, Nigeria.

The author examines the infant feeding patterns of Nigerian mothers and the possibility of formulating cheap, culturally acceptable, convenient and nutritionally adequate weaning foods based on vegetable protein sources.

253. Uzoezie, C.E. (1989) Better Life for Rural Women: The Home Economics Perspective. Paper presented at the Nigerian Vocational Association International Conference, University of Nigeria, Nsukka, 5-6 October.

This paper presented a case for home economics as a vocational subject that helps to improve the standard of living of women in rural communities in Nigeria.

254. Uzoezie, C.E. (1986) Childrearing Patterns used by Mothers and Their Children's Level of Academic Performance in Awka Local Government Area

of Anambra State. *Unpublished M.Ed Thesis.* Department of Education, University of Jos, Jos, Nigeria.

255. Women Education Branch of the F.M.E. (1989) *Blueprint on Women Education in Nigeria.* Lagos: Federal Ministry of Education, Women Education Unit.

Recommendations arising from the proceedings of the National Workshop for a Blueprint on Women Education in Nigeria, 23-26 September 1986. The recommendations covered the following: formal education, promoting science, technology and mathematics, non-formal education, women with special needs, special education for women, women education for healthy living, moral education, job opportunities, voluntary organisation/services, international organisations, legislation, research and evaluation, funding and resources, and administration and implementation.

256. Yakubu, I.L. (1991) Extension Education as an Alternative for Women Development in Nigeria. Paper presented at the International Conference on Women by the Institute of Education, University of Nigeria, Nsukka, 8-12 October.

This paper is in three segments: the definition aspect of the topic, looking at extension education as that specific act of 'teaching' adults the knowledge and skills required of a useful member of the society. The second part looks at the rural aspect of this country, approaches and process of rural development in Nigeria. The last segment discusses the extension strategies in Nigeria, its relation to community development, agriculture, cottage industries and so forth. In the conclusive part of the paper, some suggestions are offered on how to adopt this noble alternative to accelerate women's development in this country.

4

Health

257. Adekunle, L.V. (1978) Some Aspects of the Epidemiology and Sociology of Abortion. *Nigerian Behavioral Science Journal*, 1, 104-111.

258. Adekunle, Lola V. (1978) Child Immunization: What are the Impediments for Reaching Desired Goals in a Transitional Society? *Social Sciences and Medicine*, 12(5), 353-357.

This investigation aims at finding out the major impediments to the use of preventive health services in Nigeria. Immunization, one of the most important aspects of preventive health services, was used as a measure of these problems. Possible suggestions on how to improve immunizational status of children are highlighted.

259. Aden, O.O. (1986) The Relationship Between Work Capacity and Selected Measures of Physical and Physiological Variables in University of Ibadan Female Students. *Unpublished Ph.D Thesis*. Department of Health and Physical Education, University of Ibadan, Nigeria.

260. Adeyanju, F.B. (1988) Athletic Achievement and Traditional Sex-Role Conflict Among Nigerian Female Physical Education Undergraduates. *Unpublished Ph.D Thesis*. Department of Physical Education, Ahmadu Bello University, Zaria.

261. Ajayi, A.O. (1988) Iron Stores in Pregnant Nigerians and Their Infants at Term. *European Journal of Clinical Nutrition*, 42(1), 23-28.

262. Azikiwe, U. (1991) Constraints to Family Planning Practices Among Rural Women: A Case Study of a Village in Anambra State, Nigeria. Paper sent to WID Michigan State University, U.S.A., for publication.

The focus of this study was on the level of awareness and acceptability of modern family planning practices by rural women and constraints against the acceptance of the practices. The findings reveal that a majority of the women are now aware of modern family practices. Nevertheless, they are not prepared to use them due to socio-cultural and economic factors and prestige.

263. Bamisaiye, A., & Oyediran, M.A. (1983) Breast-feeding Among Female Employees at a Major Health Institution in Lagos, Nigeria. *Social Science and Medicine*, 17(23), 1867-1871.

This paper examines the breast-feeding practices of women employed at a major health institution in Lagos, Nigeria. Results show that the duration of breast-feeding was in inverse relation to salary level; women on the lowest salaries had a mean duration of breast-feeding their last child for eight months, whereas women in senior professional positions had a mean breast-feeding duration of 3.3 months. Conflicts with work responsibilities were the most commonly cited reasons for terminating breast-feeding earlier than the mother desired. It is concluded that the most satisfactory means of promoting breast-feeding among employed women is the provision of paid leave post delivery for at least three months and a provision of a creche at their place of work.

264. Basumallik, M.K., & Sengupta, J.K. (1983) Infertility in Borno Women. *Annals of Borno*, No. 1, 195-200.

This paper presents findings from the gynecological outpatients department of the University of Maiduguri Teaching Hospital, Maiduguri, on infertility.

265. Brink, P.J. (1982) Traditional Birth Attendants Among the Annang of Nigeria: Current Practices and Proposed Programmes. *Social Science and Medicine*, 16(18), 1883-1892.

This paper describes the current practices of the rural Annang traditional birth attendants (TBA), the current practices of American and Nigerian obstetrical teams, and the proposed training programme for the TBA. The paper did not attempt to cover any antenatal or postnatal practices, but is confined to the four stages of labour.

266. Caffrey, K.T. (1975) Eclampsia in Kaduna: 1969-1971. *The West African Medicinal Journal*, 23(2), 62-64.

This paper reports on the cases of eclampsia at the Ahmadu Bello University Hospital in Kaduna for a period of three years. Out of 20,694 admissions, 269 suffered from pre-eclampsia while 133 suffered eclampsia. The incidence with two percent in all hospital deliveries. Eclampsia is seen as a major obstetric emergency responsible for nearly eleven percent of maternal and eighteen percent of fetal deaths. Forty-one percent of the eclamptic patients underwent operative delivery in comparison with only nine percent of all deliveries at the hospital.

267. DiDomenico, C.M., & Asun, J.B. (1979) Breast-Feeding Practices Among Urban Women in Nigeria. In D. Raphael (ed.), *Breast-feeding and Food Policy in Hungry World*. New York: Academic Press.

This paper investigates the length and duration of breast-feeding and the knowledge, attitudes and practices of breast-feeding among different social classes of Yoruba women and other family members over the past six to ten years. Data were collected through interviews, questionnaire and focus discussion groups.

268. Dike, D.O. (1981) Influence of Significant Others and Opportunity Set on Childhood Socialization in Sports of College Female Athletes and Non-Athletes. *Unpublished M.Ed. Thesis*. Department of Health and Physical Education, University of Nigeria, Nsukka, Nigeria.

269. Ekpendu, P.E. (1984) Influence of Teachers Encouragement on Socialisation on Females into Sports in Urban and Rural Areas of Imo State. *Unpublished M.Ed. Thesis*. Department of Health and physical Education, University of Nigeria, Nsukka, Nigeria.

270. Ene, O.C. (1984) Determinants of Participation of Female Students in Sports in Colleges of Education, Anambra State. *Unpublished M.Ed. Thesis*. Department of Health and physical Education, University of Ibadan, Ibadan, Nigeria.

271. Gureje, O. (1986) Social Factors and Depression in Nigerian Women. *Acta Psychiatrica Scandinavica*, 74(4), 392-395.

272. Igun, U.A. (1982) Child-feeding Habits in a Situation of Social Change: The Case of Maiduguri, Nigeria. *Social Science and Medicine,* 16(7), 769-781.

This study sought to know the pattern of child-feeding that is emerging in a rapidly urbanizing centre, as well as the factors responsible for the emergence of the pattern. The finding is that the pattern emerging is characterized by a tendency to combine the traditional and methods learnt as a result of contact with bearers and industrial culture. Factors responsible are the mass media and the example of elite mothers whose visibly displayed adoption of bottle-feeding elevates her to the status of a fashion in the eyes of the lower income, illiterate or less educated mothers who then follow uncritically. It is suggested that more be done by the medical profession who have exhibited resigned acceptance to counter this trend in the state.

273. Ikhioya, O.S.A. (1986) Some Socio-Cultural Factors Influencing University of Ibadan Female Students Participation in Sports. *Unpublished M.Ed. Thesis.* Department of Health and Physical Education, University of Ibadan, Ibadan, Nigeria.

274. Kaine, W.N. (1976) Feeding Our Infants on the Breast: A Medical Matter of the Moment. A Year to Remember. International Women's Year Committee, University of Nigeria, Nsukka, 135-141.

The purpose of this paper is to deal with the problems of changing from breast-feeding babies to artificial feeding which is in vogue. The author highlights the advantages and disadvantages of both methods of infant feeding. Nonetheless, no matter what the advantages of artificial feeding are, breast-feeding is best for babies. Women are advised not to follow the trend in the developed countries when it comes to breast-feeding.

275. Kolo, I.A. (1991) A Survey of Awareness of Maternal Needs of Exceptional Children Amongst Nigerian Women. Paper presented at the International Conference on Women by the Institute of Education, University of Nigeria, Nsukka, 8-12 October.

This paper explains the maternal needs of exceptional children, mainly in the context of mental and physical handicapping conditions. It then reports research findings in which the awareness levels of Nigerian women of different ethnic backgrounds were rated with a researcher-designed maternal awareness rating scale. Data analysed with Mann-Whitney U test indicated a low level of awareness of special maternal needs of handicapped children amongst Nigerian women. The chi-square test revealed that no significant differences exist amongst Nigerian women given their ethnic backgrounds and relational proximity to handicapped children.

276. Kurtz, M.E.; Azikiwe, U.; Kurtz, J.C. (1992) Urban, Married Nigerian Women's Perception of Exposure to Environmental Tobacco Smoke. Paper presented at the Conference on Women in African and the African Diaspora: Bridges Across Activism and Academy held in Nigeria, West Africa in July, 13-18.

This study was designed to investigate knowledge, attitudes and preventive efforts of urban married Nigerian women in regard to exposure to environmental tobacco smoke(EST). Two hundred and forty-nine women were surveyed with a structured, written questionnaire. The results indicated that these predominantly well-educated and professionally employed Nigerian women had a fair knowledge of the adverse effects of exposure to ETS. Although their attitudes towards exposure to ETS were generally quite good, they were reluctant to take preventive measures in public. The most prominent factors relating to knowledge and attitude were age, educational level, and smoking status. Attitudes proved to be a stronger predictor of preventive efforts than knowledge.

277. Lesi, F.E.A. (1978) Infant Mortality, Diet and Disease in Nigeria. *Nigerian Medical Journal*, 8.

This paper examines the factors responsible for infant mortality, breast-feeding patterns of urban mothers, and the effect of the use of milk formula on infants.

278. Meldrum, B., and DiDomenico, C.M. (1982) Production and Reproduction; Women and Breast Feeding: Some Nigerian Examples. *Social Science and Medicine*, 16(13), 1247-1251.

This paper reviews available literature in this area in Nigeria. This is combined with a discussion of aspects of research undertaken by the authors under the headings of length of breast-feeding, bottle feeding, and fertility. Under a discussion of social and policy implications, the need for government to adopt recent WHO's code of practice to curtail the sale of artificial infant milk is stressed. It is suggested that health agencies should go to the rural areas and instruct women and men on the dangers of bottle-feeding and the benefits of breast-feeding before the 'modernization' of infant feeding, so evident in towns, spreads to the rural areas.

279. Nwakeze, P.C. (1985) Rural-Urban Differentials in Infant Mortality Rates in Nigeria: A Study of Anambra State. *Unpublished M.Sc. Thesis*. Department of Sociology/Anthropology, University of Nigeria, Nsukka, Nigeria.

This study aims at ascertaining the degree/level of rural-urban differentials in infant mortality rates and levels of infant mortality differentials based on differences in education, income, occupation, birth order, and age of mother at marriage. Findings conclude that infant mortality is significantly higher in the rural area. Suggestions are made on how to reduce infant wastage.

280. Nwana, O.C. & Ukatu, B.O. (1987) The Physical and Health Environment of the Nigerian Child as Basis for the Expanded Programme on Immunization (EPI). Paper presented at the First Annual Conference of OMEP (Organisation for Early Childhood Education), University of Nigeria, Nsukka, 20-23 May.

This paper recognises pregnancy as the first stage for preparing for the health care of the Nigerian child. It points out that the health conditions of the mother during pregnancy determines chances of survival and the personal health of the child. However, the paper reveals that at Enugu and Amechi-Awkunanaw, the available health services for Nigerian children are not maximally utilized by parents.

281. Obi, O.H. (1985) The Relationship Between Menstrual Symptomatology and Locus of Control. *Unpublished M.Sc. Thesis*. Department of Psychology, University of Nigeria, Nsukka, Nigeria.

This study investigated the relationship between menstrual symptomatology (severity of dysmenorrhea and length of menstrual period) and locus of control expectancies. There is a significant relationship between menstrual symptomatology and locus of control and personality and menstrual distress. Findings suggest that locus of control, dimension of personality alone cannot explain the psychological aetiology of menstrual symptomatology.

282. Offorma, G.C. (1992) Nigerian Women's Perception of Family Planning Practices. Paper presented at the International Conference on Women in Africa and the African Diaspora: Bridges Across Activism and Academy, Nsukka, June 12-18.

This study focuses on the attitudes of Nigerian women regarding family planning practices. The majority was found to be positive. Some suggestions were made based on the findings.

283. Ojofeitimi, E.O. (1981) Mothers' Awareness on Benefits of Breast-milk and Cultural Taboos During Lactation. *Social Science and Medicine*, 15(2), 135-138.

Two hundred and five newly delivered mothers of the two local maternity centres in Ile-Ife, Oyo state, Nigeria, were contacted after delivery to assess their levels of awareness on the importance of breast milk to infants. Things forbidden during lactation and sources of information on breast-feeding were collected by interview schedule. The levels of awareness on the importance of breast milk to infants by ages and parity of mothers were significant. However, the number of years in school versus levels of awareness were found to be significant. 88.3 percent of the mothers regarded sexual intercourse during lactation as taboo, primarily due to the fear that the infant might suck father's sperm in breast, which might cause diarrhoea. The major source of advice regarding breast-feeding are the nurses. Implications of findings for health workers in developing countries are stressed.

284. Olaseha, I.O., & Namanja, G.B. (1985-86) Focusing on Women for Water and Sanitation: The Case of Mapo Community in Ibadan, Nigeria. *International Quarterly of Community Health Education*, 6(4), 335-343.

This health service study attempts to make a needs assessment of the Mapo

Community in order to provide a basis for appropriate and meaningful interventions.

285. Olukunle, O.A. (1985) Physiological Responses of Nigerian College Females to High Intensity Exercise. *Unpublished M.Ed. Thesis*. Department of Health and Physical Education, University of Ibadan, Ibadan, Nigeria.

286. Onuoha, V.C.I. (1976) Woman and Pregnancy. *A Year to Remember*. International Women's Year Committee, University of Nigeria, Nsukka, 126-134.

This paper examined anaemia, a major problem women encounter during pregnancy. Anaemia has claimed many lives of expectant mothers and their unborn infants. The causes of the problem were discussed along with methods of prevention and treatment. The detailed discussion of causes, signs, and the implications of anaemia are very important for rural women and for planning health interventions for them.

287. Orubuloye, I.O. (1979) Sexual Abstinence Patterns in Rural Western Nigeria. Evidence from a Survey of Yoruba Women. *Social Science and Medicine*, 13(6), 667-672.

Information collected from female respondents in two rural areas of Western Nigeria suggests that traditional sexual abstinence is the main method of child-spacing, and that this is likely to remain the case for some years to come. However, a significant drop in the duration of post-partum abstinence without a corresponding increase in the adoption of modern methods of contraception may result in a significant rise in rural fertility.

288. Oyebanji, V.A. (1985) Women and Sports Participation: Facts and Fallacies. Seminar paper at Advanced Teachers College, Zaria.

289. Oyederu, O. (1986) An Evaluation of Recreation Involvement Among Female Students of Selected Teacher's Colleges in Oyo State. *Unpublished M.Sc. Thesis*. Department of Health and Physical Education, University of Ibadan, Ibadan, Nigeria.

290. Oyeyola, O.O. (1983) Some Aspects of Cyanide Metabolism in Pregnancy. *Unpublished M.Sc. Thesis.* Department of Chemistry, University of Ife, Ile-Ife, Nigeria.

In an attempt to explore the possible role of cassava in pregnancy, samples of maternal blood, foetal blood, amniotic fluid, maternal breast milk, and urine were taken from 150 pregnant women in term, and analysed for the cyanide metabolite thiocyanate (SCN). The thiocyanate contents of amniotic fluid and foetal plasma at term were 10.42 and 6.78 Mmole/lit., respectively, which may be high enough to affect the thyroid function. The thiocyanate level of the breast milk was 16.81 Mmole/lit., which passed on to the infant in the presence of insufficient iodine, may be the aetiology of endemic goitre and/or cretinism.

291. Samuel, E.S. (1983) Characteristics of Female Acceptors of Modern and Traditional Preventive Health Measures for Children in Cross River State. *Unpublished M.Ed. Thesis.* Department of Health and Physical Education, University of Nigeria, Nsukka, Nigeria.

292. Uche, G.O., Okorafor, A.E., & Okore, A.O. (1986) The Pattern of Early Menstrual Cycles in Nigerian Girls. *Annals of Human Biology,* 13(1), 83-86.

A total of 2,528 recorded menstrual cycles were collected from 422 girls in schools in Enugu and Nsukka in Anambra State, Nigeria. The mean and standard deviation for all cycles were 30.9 and 18.60 days respectively. The result supports the findings from other parts of the world that menstrual cycles are highly irregular during the first few years after menarche and that the variability of those cycles decreases as menstrual life continues. A comparison between the study and others done in North America and Europe suggests that socioeconomic development, with its attendant improvement in nutrition and the elimination of infectious diseases, may be helping to bring about a reduction in variability of early menstrual cycles.

293. Ugwuegbu, D.C.E., & Ogundeyin, W.M. (1977) Self-Image and Job Satisfaction of the Nigerian Nurse: A Comparative Study. *Journal of Advanced Nursing,* Vol. 2, 29-39.

This study is a comparison between the professional and student nurses as it pertains to self-image and job satisfaction. Areas which need improvement in the nursing profession were pointed out.

294. Uwaegbute, A.C. (1987) Infant Feeding Practices of Nigerians and Ghanian Women Living in the Guelph-Kitchener-Waterloo Area. *Unpublished M.Sc. Thesis*. Faculty of Graduate Studies, The University of Guelph, Canada.

The infant feeding practices by the two groups of women are assessed in Canada and in their home countries. The children's medical history, heights and weights, and food intake were also examined. It was found that there was a significant difference between the method of early infant feeding selected in Canada and in their home countries. Custom was the main factor influencing their choice of an early infant feeding method at home, while convenience was the main reason in Canada.

295. Uwaegbute, A.C., & Amazigo, U. (1990) Igbo Women in Health and Nutrition. Paper Presented at the Seminar on Igbo Women in Socio-Economic Change. Better Life Programme (Imo State Wing) Owerri/Institute of African Studies, University of Nigeria, Nsukka, 3-5 April.

The relationship between health and nutrition is established before discussing the contributions of Igbo women to the society.

296. Uyanga, J. (1980) Rural-Urban Differences in Child Care and Breast-feeding Behaviour in Southeastern Nigeria. *Social Science and Medicine*, 14(1), 23-29.

A model of household behaviour is used to test some postulates concerning the effects of markets and non-market roles of urban and rural women on childcare breast-feeding. This paper analyses the determinants of total child care time for pre-school children and explores the allocative effects and intra-household substitutions that took place. This is used to explain the casual relationships behind rural-urban variations in breast-feeding behaviour. The results suggest the significance of income, education, job compatibility, and household demographic structure, and point to human capital change as a relevant policy parameter.

297. Uzodike, A.A. (1986) Teachers' Roles in Socialising Urban and Rural Federal Secondary School Students in Sports in Enugu, Anambra State, Nigeria. *Unpublished M.Ed. Thesis.* Department of Health and physical Education, University of Ibadan, Ibadan, Nigeria.

5

Home and Family

298. Acholonu, R. (1990) Women, Love and Marriage in the Igbo Traditional Novel: A Paradigm of Pragmatic and Dynamic Living. Paper presented at the Seminar on Igbo Women in Socio-Economic Change. Better Life Programme (Imo State Wing) Owerri/Institute of African Studies, University of Nigeria, Nsukka, 3-5 April.

This study critically analyses selected texts that assess the artistic realisation of the traditional couple's quest for selfhood and fulfilment by way of love and marriage. The paper focuses attention on the woman's status, role and expectation vis-à-vis her concept of love, marriage and happiness. This is done by seeking answers to seven questions.

299. Adegbola, O. (1987) *Regional and Socio-Economic Fertility Differentials in Nigeria,* 1981-1982. Brussels, Belgium: Vrije Universiteit Brussel, Interuniversity Programme in Demography (IPD) Working Paper No. 1987.

300. Adeokun, L.A. (1982) Marital Sexual Relationships and Birth Spacing Among Two Yoruba Subgroups. *Africa,* 52(4), 1-14.

301. Adeokun, L.A. (1983) Marital Sexuality and Birth Spacing Among the Yoruba. In C. Oppong (ed.), *Female and Male in West Africa.*

302. Adewuyi, A.A. (1983) Rural-Urban Fertility Differential in Southern Nigeria: A Review. *Odu,* 23, 122-132.

303. Afigbo, A.E. (1974-75) Culture and Fertility Among the Igbo of Nigeria: A Historical Investigation. Igbo Standardization and Culture Seminars. Collection of papers read, reports and conclusions reached at the two annual seminars held in University of Nigeria, Nsukka, organised by the Society for Promoting Igbo Language and Culture. Igbo Language Development Series No. 2. Onitsha: Varsity Press for the Society for Promoting Igbo Language and Culture.

This paper seeks to highlight those cultural factors that influence fertility among the Igbo in the pre-colonial period. How these have been undermined or re-informed by the impact of western ideas, techniques and practices is discussed.

304. Ajayi, S.L. (1991) A Comparative Analysis of Gender Roles in the House Among Rural and Urban Areas. Paper presented at the International Conference on Women by the Institute of Education, University of Nigeria, Nsukka, 8-12 October.

The performing of household tasks were studied among 192 homemakers on the campus of the Ahmadu Bello University, Zaria, and in nearby Shika Village. Results of the study show that a significant proportion of the household tasks, such as food preparation, food serving, cleaning up used kitchen utensils, washing of children and other family clothings, budgeting, physical care of children, teaching and coaching children, and the collecting of water were performed by the majority (77.1-94.5%) of respondents from Ahmadu Bello University quarters, Zaria. On the other hand, food preparation and sewing, cleaning used kitchen utensils, washing of children and other family clothing were the activities performed by the majority (54-94%) of respondents residing in Shika Village.

305. Akinkoye, O. (1984) Attitude to Child-bearing by Single Nigerian Women. *Nigerian Journal of Economic and Social Studies,* 26(1), 135-142.

306. Alabi, J.A. (1984) Parents-in-law Problems in Nigerian Marriage. *Unpublished M.Ed. Thesis.* Department of Education, University of Ibadan, Ibadan, Nigeria.

This study examines the influence that parents-in-law exert on Nigerian homes (marriages) using 200 married men and women. Two out of three hypotheses were rejected.

307. Aluko, G.B., & Alfa, M.O. (1985) Marriage and Family. In WIN (ed.), *Women in Nigeria Today.* London: Zed Book Ltd., 163-173.

This paper defined and discussed some key concepts: family, marriage, housewife, inheritance, and division of labour. The focus of the paper is the study of four couples (two elite and two non-elite families) to reinforce the fact that women are exploited and subjugated to their husbands. It concludes that exploitation and subjugation of women is not a class phenomenon but a gender phenomenon; women are not treated as equals in the house.

308. Alti-Muazu, M. (1985) Hausa Traditional Birth Practices and the Health of Mother and Child. In WIN (ed.), *Women in Nigeria Today*. London: Zed Book Ltd., 178-186.

This paper reveals some shocking birth practices that are very hazardous to both mother and child. Practices vividly discussed are confinement period, post-natal period, post-natal diet, practices performed on the new baby, naming ceremony, baby's diet and visits. The problem, according to the paper, is illiteracy. Thus, women should be informed of the advantages of attending ante- and post-natal clinics. Traditional birth attendants (TBD) should be taught the importance of sterilization of their instruments. The enlightenment should be through the mass media, adult classes, and other public places.

309. Ama, I.O. (1985) Internal Migration and Fertility Behaviour in Edda Clan of Afikpo L.G.A., Imo State: A Comparative Fertility Survey of Migrants and Non-migrants. *Unpublished M.Sc. Thesis*. Department of Sociology/Anthropology, University of Nigeria, Nsukka, Nigeria.

The fertility differential between migrant and non-migrant women of Edda origin was the focus of this study. It also aimed at finding the influences of internal migration and other cultural norms on the fertility behaviour of the women. It concludes that internal migration tends to have some effect on fertility behaviour of Edda women. Recommendations are made to check the incidence of high fertility rate among non-migrant women.

310. Amechi, E.E. (1981) Woman-to-Woman Marriage: Its Legal Significance. AMAN: *Journal of Society, Culture and Environment,* 1(1), 20-35.

This paper discussed the various forms of woman-to-woman marriage as practised in Igboland. Using specific cases, the legality of the practice is proven.

311. Anyanwu, G.A. & Iloeje, I.C. (1991) Adolescents Perceptions of Gender's Role in the Family. Paper presented at the International Conference on Women by the Institute of Education, University of Nigeria, Nsukka, 8-12 October.

Family instability is the main cause of the present societal instability. Role performance in the home consequently affects family stability. If individuals in the home are aware and perform their roles, conflicts and stress in the home will be reduced to a significant degree, thereby ensuring family and societal stability. This study then aims at examining the following: adolescents role expectations for wives and husbands in the present and future homes; if their perception of role specialization in the home of the future is based on gender, or career; and if they expect role diffusion in the home of the future. The study population is adolescents in the Nsukka Local Government Area. Sample size is 300 adolescents aged (17-21) years, comprising 100 university undergraduates, 100 artisan apprentices and 100 business/traders. Data were collected using structured questionnaire, self administered for the educated and scheduled interview for the illiterates. Variance, mean and critical ratio were applied for analysis of data. The findings should be used for planning educational programmes for the youths, especially in the area of social and family life studies.

312. Aweda, D.A. (1984) Sex-role inequality in the African Family. Contemporary Implications for Policy. *Ife Social Sciences Review*, 7 (1 & 2), 183-197.

The paper examines the theoretical basis of sex-role inequality, viz the allocation of sex-roles, the perception of the females about their sex roles, and policy implications for sex-role equality.

313. Azokwu, W.N. (1989) Utilization of dehulled cowpeas by Onitsha Women. *Unpublished B.Sc. Thesis*. Department of Food Technology and Home Sciences, University of Nigeria, Nsukka.

314. Azikiwe, U., (1992) Widowhood Practices in Nigeria: Case of Afikpo Community. Paper presented at the International Conference on Women in Africa and the African Diaspora: Bridges Across Activism and Academy held in Abuja Nigeria, West Africa, in June.

This study investigated the widowhood practices in a matrilineal community, Afikpo. Two hundred and ten (210) widows were used and the instruments for collecting data included a focus group discussion (FCD) technique and the questionnaire. Some differences exist in widowhood practices between Afikpo community and other parts of Igbo land; culture/tradition are responsible for the perpetration of the oppressive practices; and compliance with those inhuman practices is based on superstition. It is suggested that federal, state and governing body in Afiko 'Esa' should enact laws to abolish those oppressive and dehumanizing practices.

315. Badekale-Sunmonu, J. (1992) Gender, Development and Peace. Paper presented at the International Conference on Peace Education, University of Nigeria, Nsukka, 6-9 May.

This paper examines the issue of gender as it relates to development and peace in Nigeria. The paper highlights the fact that women, as part of the gender issue, need to be more recognised as contributors to development in order to maintain peace. It also examined the interrelationship of gender, peace and development. Recommendations are made for the involvement of both gender in development and the maintenance of peace.

316. Bassey, A.J. (1987) Fertility Differentials in the Cross River State of Nigeria and Their Economic Implications. *Unpublished Ph.D. Thesis*. Department of Economics, University of Nigeria, Nsukka, Nigeria.

This investigation examines the extent to which incomes of household, educational levels of women, marital status of women, age of women and the religion of women explain fertility differences in the state. Apart from age, income and education affect fertility.

317. Burfisher, M.E., & Horenstein, N.R. (1985) Sex Roles in the Nigerian Tiv Farm Household. *Women's Roles and Gender Differences in Development*. West Hartford: Kumarian Press.

This study focuses on the division of labour, income, and financial obligations among the Tivs and the implications of these divisions to development projects.

The authors stress that the concept of women's role in development needs to be perceived for what it is: an important productivity issue that should be a standard part of the planning process. They conclude that if the goal of development is ultimately the integration of both men and women, then different needs and incentives of each must be explicitly recognised and addressed so that projects and programme can become responsive to the people they are designed to assist.

318. Caldwell, J.C. (1977) The Economic Rationality of High Fertility: An Investigation Illustrated with Nigerian Survey Data. *Population Studies*, 31(1), 5-28.

This paper argues that large family size will continue to be upheld because of the values and practices of the people. Children are the most valuable thing among Nigerians.

319. Caldwell, J.C. (1978) Marriage, the Family and Infertility in Sub-Saharan Africa with Special Reference to Research Programmes in Ghana and Nigeria. *Family and Marriage in Some African and Asiatic Countries*. Cairo: Cairo Demographic Centre, Research Monograph Series, No. 6, 359-371.

This paper reports investigations in Ghana and Nigeria in 1962-64 and 1973 respectively. It examines monogamy and polygyny, age at first marriage, relationship between the married state and exposure to conception, and nature of the family and family economics. It suggests that much of the traditional family and marriage survive more than the contemporary marriage and family.

320. Chojnacka, H. (1978) Polygyny and the Rate of Population Growth. *Human Resources Research Bulletin*. No. 78/05, Lagos: University of Lagos.

One hundred and thirty households of selected communities in the Southern belt of Nigeria were used for the study. The research compared monogamous and polygynous unions on demographic and socioeconomic variables. Polygynous unions prevailed amongst farmers, petty traders, manual workers, Moslems, and traditional believers. Furthermore, lower level of educational attainment, lower standards of living, and higher child mortality rate are prevalent among polygynous households. One important finding is the absence of any significant difference between the wives in the two types of unions with respect to completed fertility. The paper concludes that the major demographic consequence of practising polygyny is reflected in the very young nuptiality patterns for females, which directly affects the rate of population growth.

321. Davies, C.B. (1986) Motherhood in the Works of Male and Female Igbo Writers: Achebe, Emecheta, Nwapa and Nzekwu. In C.B. Davies et al. (eds.), *Ngambi pl 2 Women in Africa Literature.* Trenton: New Jersey: African World Press.

322. Dike, C.H. (1982) A Socioeconomic Analysis of Nigerian Fertility Pattern. *Unpublished M.Sc. Thesis.* Department of Economics, University of Nigeria, Nsukka, Nigeria. 162 pp.

The data used for this study are from fertility and allied surveys and national population census figures of 1963. The author examines the effects of age of mother, level of education, place of residence, type of marital union and religion, and the general mores of the people on fertility. Age varied directly with number of children. There is also a fertility convergence between urban and rural women, and the cultural norms and the social mores favour many children.

323. Edegbai, B. (1986) The Views of Working Mothers on Why Some Mothers do not Breast-Feed Their Babies. *Unpublished M.Ed. Thesis.* Department of Health and Physical Education, University of Ibadan, Ibadan, Nigeria.

324. Ekechukwu, S.I.C. (1984) Determinants of Late Age of Marriage Among Literate Females of Imo State. *Unpublished M.Ed. Thesis.* Department of Education, University of Ibadan, Ibadan, Nigeria.

This study set out to identify the factors that cause delay in marriage among literate females and also the degree of which identified factors contribute to the delay. It also compared the opinions of the subjects in terms of sex, marital status, and age for any significant difference with regard to five selected factors derived theoretically from some of the generated items. Sex significant factors labelled high social status, economic and social security, improved life style, cultural factors, selective factors, and marital cost factors were the main causes derived from the data. There were significant sex marital status and age differences in the opinion of subject regarding some of the five selected variables.

325. Ekefre, A.N. (1984) Akuho 'Fattening' Institution in Cross River State: Implications for Social and Sex Role Guidance. *Unpublished M.A. Thesis.* Department of Education, University of Ife, Ile-Ife, Nigeria.

The cultural aspects of the institution, the processes involved, and the type of counselling procedures used are discussed. Data were collected through questionnaire administered to 110 female participants, 10 instructors, and 50 male adults; interview and observation were used as well. The findings show that 'fattening' represents a period during which a girl is given comprehensive lessons and guidance on house-keeping, marriage, sex and social roles. The counselling carried out is eclectic. It is suggested that the use of local languages be incorporated into modern African counselling practices.

326. Eruchalu, U.O. (1986) Child Survival Prospects and Fertility Among Rural Igbo Women: A Case Study of Nnobi. *Unpublished B.Sc. Thesis.* Department of Sociological/Anthropology, University of Nigeria, Nsukka, Nigeria.

327. Esekire, A.E. (1986) The Effect of Work Outside the Home on Female Sex Roles in Marriage and Family in Benin City. *Unpublished M.Ed. Thesis.* Department of Education, University of Benin, Benin City, Nigeria.

328. Eze, O., & Nwebo, O.E. (1989) Widowhood Practices: Law and Custom. *Widowhood Practices in Imo State.* Proceedings of the Better Life Programme for Rural Women Workshop held at Owerri, 6-7 June, 60-69.

This paper argues that the handicaps of Igbo widows in their rights of inheritance, especially in relation to land, was always based on law and custom. However, the authors conclude that the various forms of discriminatory oppression of our women (particularly the widows) under our laws and customs are dehumanizing and debasing to womanhood, unconscionable, unjust, and unconstitutional. An important issue raised in the paper is that legislation is not enough to erase human prejudices and entrenched behaviour. The solution, according to the authors, lies in putting into practical terms the legalistic and theoretical suggestions that can make our people change age-old practices and patterns of behaviour.

329. Fadeyi, T.O. (1987) Participatory Behaviour as a Factor in the Family Planning Programme in Ibadan City. *Unpublished M.Ed. Thesis*. Department of Education, University of Ibadan, Ibadan, Nigeria.

330. Farooq, G.M. (1980) Household Fertility Decision-Making in Nigeria. Working Paper No. 75a, Geneva, ILO.

This study was conducted in four state of former Southwestern Nigeria using a sample of 3,013 households. The woman's level of educational attainment is among the socioeconomic factors relevant to household fertility decision-making. It was also observed that the attitude to family limitation was positive when couples had achieved a sufficient number of live births.

331. Fatunla, G.T. (1991) Report on the Baseline Survey for the UNFPA Integrated Women Development Project in Ondo State.

332. Fawunmi, F.E. (1987) The Changing Roles of Women in the Nigerian Society. Paper presented at the Seminar on Women's Studies: The State of the Art Now in Nigeria by the Women's Research and Documentation Centre (WORDOC), Institute of African Studies, University of Ibadan, 4-6 November.

333. Federal Republic of Nigeria (1982) The Nigerian Fertility Survey 1981/81: Principal Report, Methodology and Findings, Vol. 1.

334. Igboeli, C.C. (1984) A Study of the Knowledge and Practices of Rural Mothers of Obimo Village in the Nsukka L.G.A. of Anambra State on Antenatal Care and the Immunization of Their Children. *Unpublished M.Ed. Thesis*. Department of Health and physical Education, University of Nigeria, Nsukka, Nigeria.

335. Ilori, P.A. (1976) Factors Determining Rural-Urban Fertility Differentials in Western Nigeria. A Case Study of Ife, Ilesha and Selected Rural Areas in Oyo Province. A Research Report Submitted to the Department of Demography

and Social Statistics, University of Ife, Ile-Ife.

336. Imonikebe, B. (1993) Strategies for Meeting Family Food Needs in a Depressed Economy: Implications for Vocational Home Economics Education. Nigerian Vocational Journal: NVA. VI, November, 48-54.

The purpose of this study is to identify the measures that homemakers adopted in coping with the high cost of feeding. A total of 330 housewives in Benin City were involved in the study. Findings showed that planning of meals before shopping, buying of foodstuffs in bulk, eating more foods in season, practising home gardening, engaging in subsistence farming, making use of storage facilities such as deep freezers, fridges, and tins, were the major practices adopted by families in meeting their food needs.

337. Iro, M.I. (1978) Social Correlates of Divorce Among Lagos Elites Who Married in Nigeria. In C. Oppong et al. (eds.), *Marriage, Fertility and Parenthood in West Africa*. Canberra: Australian National University, 399-406.

338. Iro, M.I. (1975) Social Research and Its Application to Policy: A Critique of Studies in Nigeria. Paper presented at the Conference on Social Research and National Development in Nigeria, University of Ibadan, 28 September-4 October.

This paper criticises the use of data from census and court records as very inadequate when used as bases for studying divorce issues, while neglecting social demographic and economic determinants.

339. Isyaku, D.M. (1981) Study of Utilization of Time in Household Activities in Borno Village. *Unpublished B.Ed. Thesis*. Department of Education, Ahmadu Bello University, Zaria.

340. Kalu, W.J. (1990) Motherhood Concept Among Igbo Women. Paper presented at the Seminar on Igbo Women in Socioeconomic Change, Better Life Programme (Imo State Wing) Owerri/Institute of African Studies, University of Nigeria, Nsukka, 3-5 April.

This paper examines the motherhood concept in contemporary Igbo women, the relationship to traditional perspectives, and the recognition of its social and economic functions.

341. Kalu, W.J. (1989) Motherhood Role in Married Female Undergraduate Students. *Nigerian Journal of Counselling and Development,* Vol. 4, 100-113.

342. Kalu, W.J. (1987) Childbearing Experiences of Contemporary Nigerian Working Mothers. *Women Studies International Forum,* 10(2) 141-156.

343. Kanu, V.A. (1989) A Study of the Causes and Consequences of Divorce in Arochukwu Community. *Unpublished Diploma in Social Work Project.* Department of Sociology/Anthropology, University of Nigeria, Nsukka.

344. Kisekka, M.N. (1980) Marital and Familial Patterns in Zaria, Nigeria. *Africana Marburgensia* 2,

This paper attempts to portray the marital patterns of the sample. Eighty-four percent had a polygamous family background, while 58 percent were mainly monogamous marriages. However, this pattern changes as the men grow older. The paper also looked at family size, preference of sex of the child, religion of spouses, sexual attitude. Birth control and abortion were regarded with disfavour.

345. Kolo, I.A. & Garba, A. (1991) Perception of Women in Training Centres of Sex-role in Kano State of Nigeria. Paper presented at the International Conference on Women by the Institute of Education, University of Nigeria, Nsukka, 8-12 October.

This paper is a study of how women receiving vocational training in designated women centres in Kano State perceive of stereotypical sex and androgynous work role typings prevalently believed in typical Hausa communities. Researcher-designed Occupational Sex Role Typing Scale was administered on one hundred and sixty women receiving male and female sex typed occupational training. Analysis of data indicated that choice of occupational training type by women was significantly contingent upon sex-role perception of occupations. It was also found that perception of women who participated in the study was still significantly towards traditional sex-role typings as against the need for emphasizing androgynous work-role typing amongst the women folk. The paper, therefore, strongly recommends the infusion of formal vocational guidance not only in the vocational training centres involving women, but also in the efforts at education and better life programmes for women.

346. Lambo, T.A., and Bakare, C.G.M. (1981) The Psychological Dimension of Fertility: An Intensive Study in Western Nigeria. *Rural Africana*, 14, 82-88.

347. Lovejoy, P.E. (1988) Concubinage and the Status of Women Slaves in Early Colonial Northern Nigeria. *Journal of African History*, 29(2), 245-266.

348. Mann, Kistin (1985) *Marrying Well: Marriage, Status and Social Change Among the Educated Elite in Colonial Lagos.* London and New York: Cambridge University Press, 194 pp.

This historical study analyses the changes that have taken place in the institution of marriage among the educated elite in Lagos during the late nineteenth and early twentieth centuries. The book revealed that men and women responded quite differently to the new marriage laws and customs. Elite men profited more than women from access to western education, professions and occupation. Elite women, on the other hand, more willingly embraced the British Christian practice of monogamy, though its ideas tended to make them more dependent. The result of this new approach to marriage was unstable and flexible marriage among the elite.

349. Martin, S. (1984) Gender and Innovation: Farming, Cooking and Palm Processing in the Ngwa Region, Southeastern Nigeria 1900-1930. *Journal of African History*, 25, 411-427.

350. McCarthy, J., & Oni, G.A. (1987) Desired Family Size and Its Determinants Among Urban Nigerian Women: A Two-Stage Analysis. *Demography*, 24(2), 279-290.

351. Mohammed, S.I. (1985) Women, The Family and the Wider Society. In Imam Proceedings of the Second Annual Women in Nigeria Conference, Zaria, 47-60.

352. Muller, Jean-Claude (1978) On Bridewealth and Meaning Among the Rukuba, Plateau State, Nigeria. *Africa,* 48(2), 161-175.

Bridewealth and its function are discussed. Payment varied considerably from case to case.

353. National Population Bureau (1984) The Nigerian Fertility Survey 1981/82. Principal Report, Methodology and Findings Vol. 1.

354. Nwachukwu, D. (1991) Field Study on Widowhood in Nigeria. *Amka.* An Occasional Newsletter of the Biennial Institute of African Women in Religion and Culture. Issue No. 1., 66-71.

This study was carried out in a clinical setting using indepth interview, participant and obtrusive observation, case study analysis, and questionnaire techniques.

355. Nwadinobi, A. (1988) Causes and Effect of Divorce in Umuahia Urban, Imo State. *Unpublished Diploma in Social Work Project.* Department of Sociology/Anthropology, University of Nigeria, Nsukka.

356. Nwoga, D.I. (1989) Widowhood Practices: The Imo State Experience. *Widowhood Practices in Imo State.* Proceedings of the Better Life Programme (BLP) for Rural Women Workshop, Owerri, 6-7 June, 32-40.

This paper discusses specific aspects of widowhood practices in Imo State and the rationale behind them. The author also discusses a number of interesting factors that could bring about change: white-collar employment for the widow that can necessitate her non-compliance with the one year period of mourning at home; movement towards individualism and the nuclear family; role of traditional rulers in influencing local changes; and the enactment of new laws of inheritance.

357. Nzewi, E. (1989) Widowhood Practices: A Female Perspective. *Widowhood Practices in Imo State.* Proceedings of the Better Life Programme (BLP) for Rural Women Workshop, Owerri, 6-7 June, 43-57.

This paper highlights the problems of women and widows backed-up with statistical data. The State was divided into four zones and the discussion reveals some differences between the zones. Factors which affect widowhood practices in the state include socioeconomic status of women, religion, women's educational level, occupation, the relationship between women and their husbands, and the relationship between women and their relatives-in-laws, particularly the females (umuada).

358. Okore, A.O. (1977) The Value of Children Among Ibo Households in Nigeria: A Study of Arochukwu Division and Urban Umuahia in Imo State. *Unpublished Ph.D. Dissertation.* Australian National University.

This study set out to identify, analyse, and explain the various meanings attached to childbearing by the Ibos. The results reveal that fertility is high among the sample (an average of 7-8 children ever born). The desire for additional children is pervasive despite the expressed awareness of the increasing cost of raising children. The extended family base generally tends to cushion some of the hardships that should have otherwise been attendant on the large family size.

359. Okoro, C.I. (1990) Nutrition Knowledge, Attitudes and Practices of Owerri Mothers. *Unpublished M.Sc. Thesis.* Department of Food Technology and Home Sciences, University of Nigeria, Nsukka.

360 Olorunfemi, A.M.O. (1987) Family Planning and Contraceptive Attitude and Practice in Rural Communities: Case Study of Selected Communities. *Unpublished M.Ed. Thesis.* Department of Education, University of Ibadan, Ibadan, Nigeria.

361. Omideyi, A.K. (1985) Natural Fertility and Fertility Levels in Nigeria. *Ife Social Sciences Review*, 8(1 and 2), 102-125.

The aim of the paper is to determine how Nigeria's natural fertility compares with empirical/maximum levels and to discuss the factors responsible for divergences between natural fertility and fertility levels in Nigeria.

362. Omideyi, A.K. (1983) The Persistence of High Fertility in Eastern Nigeria: An Analysis Based on a Simple Survey of Married Women in 1971-72.

Unpublished Ph.D. Dissertation. University of London.

363. Onuora, V.I. (1976) Graduate Marriage: How Successful? *A Year to Remember*. International Women's Year Committee, University of Nigeria, Nsukka, 30-37.

This paper gave a brief summary of the status of a woman and her role in a traditional marriage. A lot of changes have taken place in the married lives of educated women. The failure of most graduate marriages was associated with stress resulting from the complexity of the society, interference by in-laws, rather than level of education. The author believes that a marriage of graduates is more stable than when the woman is an illiterate. The paper advised men that the days of master/servant relationships are gone and that a stable marriage is built on a relationship of equals, adaptation, consideration for one another, and tolerance.

364. Oppong, C.; Adaba, G.; Bekombo-Priso, M.; & Mogey, J. (1978) *Marriage, Fertility and Parenthood in West Africa*. Canberra: The Australian National University.

Two volumes of papers were presented at the XVth Seminar of the International Sociology Association Committee on Family Research, Lome, Togo in 1976.

Volume 1:

Part 1 - Family and marriage systems (covering the whole of West Africa).
Part 2 - Parents, children, and childcare: a general study on the changing economic roles of children in a comparative perspective.
Part 3 - Family system and change (Bete, Nigeria, Ghana).

Volume 2:

Part 4 - Factors affecting fertility, in addition to some general studies (Nigeria, Ghana, Ivory coast).
Part 5 - Family planning and birth control (Nigeria, Sierra Leone).

365. Oyebola, D.D.O. (1981) Yoruba Traditional Healers Knowledge of Contraception, Abortion and Infertility. *East African Medical Journal,* 58, 777-785.

366. Pittin, R.I. (1986) The Control of Reproduction: Principle and Practice in Nigeria. *Review of African Political Economy,* No. 35, 40-53.

367. Pittin, R.I. (1979) Marriage and Alternative Strategies: Marriage Patterns of Hausa Women in Katsina City. *Unpublished Ph.D. Dissertation.* The School of Orientatal and African Studies, London: University of London.

This study investigated the strategies employed to weaken male domination by Hausa women. The literature on Hausa women, which ignored the *ja ara a* (women who do not marry), is said to be sexist. The theoretical framework of the study is a great contribution to the study of Muslim women.

368. Singha, P. & Verma, O.P. (1982) Fertility Pattern of Muslim Hausa Women in Northern Nigeria. *The Nigerian Journal of Economic and Social Studies*, 24(1), March, 185-198.

This paper attempts to bring out the relevant fertility information of Muslim Hausa women in Malumfashi. The study covered 302 Hausa-speaking households. Some of the findings include: fertility rate with Muslim-Hausa population is lower than the national average; polygamous marriage gives lower fertility than monogamous ones; polygamy afforded relative higher marital instability than monogamy; and a high incidence of venereal diseases in this area, which may be a contributory factor in the sterility of a high proportion of the women.

369. Solamone, F.A. (1976) The Arrow and the Bird: Proverbs in the Solution of Hausa Conjugal Conflicts. Journal of Anthropological Research, 32, 358-371.

This paper examines the context and conjugal conflicts among Hausa couples. The use of proverbs by the couples to challenge or assert sexual prowess and how this is used to resolve conflicts at home is discussed.

370. Solanke, F. (1977) Abortion: A Legal Perspective. *Nigerian Medical*

Journal, June, 7-9.

The author identifies two defects in the Nigerian Law on abortion: the inability to distinguish between abortion performed by a qualified doctor and a quack; and ambiguity as to what constitutes lawful and unlawful procurement of abortion. There is a call for legal reforms to clarify the ambiguities as well as for liberalization of the abortion law.

371. Udoye, E.C. (1986) A Study of the Influence of Sex, Marriage and Education on Attitude Towards Women's Role in Nigerian Society. *Unpublished M.Sc. Thesis.* Department of Psychology, University of Nigeria, Nsukka, Nigeria.

The results show that marriage had a significant effect on attitude towards women's role, while sex and education had no significant effect on attitude towards women's role in society. The overall result shows a stereotype and traditional attitude towards women's role.

372. Ukaegbu, A.O. (1978) Family Size Preferences of Spouses in Rural Eastern Nigeria. *Population and Development.*

This paper discusses the reasons why parents long for large numbers of children. Children are more valuable than wealth. Power and influence of any household depends upon the number of their male members. Children are special gifts from God and they are not given to anyone who wants them. Children will earn income and thus take good care of their parents. Family responsibilities are made easier since there are many people in the family to share them. Many children is an assurance of a grand and decent burial.

373. Ukaegbu, A.O. (1977) Family Planning Attitudes and Practices in Rural Eastern Nigeria. S.F.P., 8(7) July.

374. Ukaegbu, A.O. (1976) Marriage and Fertility in East Central Nigeria: A Case Study of the Ngwa Igbo Women. *Unpublished Ph.D. Dissertation.* University of London.

375. Uku, P.E.B. (1986) *25 Years of Partnership*. Benin City: Bendel Newspaper Corporation, 114 pp.

This book is a memoir of the author's marriage. It contains the contributions of the author in women's development programmes. This is a story of a successful, cooperative family with many observations about the organisational efforts required to manage an extended family household and demanding careers.

376. Umeh, O. (1987) Women, Marriage and Child-Rearing in Igbo Traditional Poetry. Paper presented at the 2nd Annual Seminar on Igbo Life and Culture, University of Nigeria, Nsukka, 1-4 December.

This paper reveals that marriage and child-rearing are closely linked in the Igbo traditional society, and that poems on the occasion of marriage are often sung on the occasion of childbirth. The woman is solely responsible for infertility in marriage while the man is never thought of as a possible cause for infertility.

377. Unuigbe, J.A. (1988) Genital Factors with Tetanus in Nigerian Women. *Jouranl of the Royal Society of Health*, 108(2), 62-63.

378. Uwaegbute, A.C. (1987) Infant Feeding Patterns and Comparative Assessment of Formulated Weaning Foods Based on Vegetable Proteins. *Unpublished Ph.D. Dissertation*. Department of Food Technology and Home Science, University of Nigeria, Nsukka.

379. Uyanga, J. (1980) The Value of Children and Childbearing in Rural Southeastern Nigeria. *Rural Africana*, No. 7, Spring, 37-54.

This paper examines the values that Nigerian parents attach to their children and how this tends to affect their reproductive behaviour. The study collected data from 600 rural wives and husbands. Results reveal that with the current level of reproduction and socioeconomic circumstance, children provide no economic and social benefits to rural households. Rural women are very reluctant to cease childbearing even when they have reached the end of their reproductive age.

6

Labour Forces and Work Place

380. Aboyade, B. (1988) Barriers to Participation of Nigerian Women in Modern Labour Force. In Ogunsheye (ed.), *Nigerian Women and Development*. Ibadan: Ibadan University press.

381. Adebayo, C.O. (1980) Study Utilization of Time by Working-Class Women. *Unpublished B.Ed. Thesis*. Department of Education, Ahmadu Bello University, Zaria.

382. Adewuyi, A.A. (1980) Childcare and Female Employment in a Nigerian Metropolis. The Role of the Under Six's. *The Nigerian Journal of Economics and Social Studies,* 22(2), July, 197-218.

The author examined the influence of family composition on the employment of mothers. In particular, the study looked at the employment pattern of mothers by the age of the youngest child in the household. The findings include: employment rates of mothers by the age of the youngest children is high when compared with labour force participation of women from many parts of the world; the employment rate of mothers does not increase once the youngest child enters school.

383. Agheyisi, R.U. (1985) The Labour Market Implications of the Access of Women to Higher Education in Nigeria. In WIN (ed.), *Women in Nigeria Today.* London: Zed Book Ltd., 143-156.

This paper attempts to present the true picture of the labour market in Nigeria with a clear division between male and female occupations. Its implications on the access of women to higher education were discussed. The barriers facing women in the labour market are grouped into direct discrimination, indirect discrimination, and educational opportunities and socialization. Finally, the paper is organised into three sections: overview of the Nigerian labour market and female involvement in it, data on the pattern of female participation in University education, and conclusions.

384. Aina, O.I. (1984) Women in Business: A Study of Female Entrepreneurs

in Southwestern Nigeria.

The study focuses on female entrepreneurs in Southwest Nigeria. The main purpose is to identify the factors that led to their emergence, as well as examine factors that inhibit their performance as owners of capital and employers of labour.

385. Akinbode, A., & Akande, B.E. (1987) The Situation of Rural Women in Nigeria. *Rural Sociologist,* 7(3), 210-215.

386. Anyanwu, G.A., & Nwanjinba, C.U. (1991) Farm and Non-Farm Activities of Rural Women: Their Perception of Their Career Opportunity and Constraints. Paper presented at the International Conference on Women by the Institute of Education, University of Nigeria, Nsukka, 8-12 October.

One hundred women from an equal number of farm families were sampled from four villages in two local government areas in Imo State, Nigeria. Care was taken to ensure that the women were active participants in family farm and non-farm activities. Well-trained enumerators were selected to administer the interview schedules that had been prepared and validated. Data were analyzed using descriptive statistics. The following are some of the findings: (1) a large proportion of rural women have little or no education; (2) a significant proportion of rural women in Imo State have no formal skills training in non-farm profession and no formal training in farming skills; (3) farming is the only activity that all rural women in Imo State engage in; (4) the women perceived inadequate education and lack of requisite training as constituting the most important constraint in engaging in preferred profession; (5) a majority of the women agree that they are satisfied with farming though they would rather be engaged in other activities; (6) although the women engage in farming activities, a majority of the rural women do not want to be called farmers or housewives. The major recommendations made are to provide skills training and effective extension services in Agriculture and Home Economics for rural women.

387. Arowolo, O.O. (1978) Female Labour Force Participation and Fertility. The Case of Ibadan City in the Western States of Nigeria. In Oppong, C. et al. (eds.), *Marriage, Fertility and Parenthood in West Africa.* Canberra: Australian University Press.

Based on the rural-urban background differences in the women studied in 1977, the author arrived at the negative association between active participation in the labour force and fertility among Ibadan-born women. The author found that among the women studied, higher levels of education were associated with higher fertility among women of rural origin, while post-primary education appeared to reduce fertility of Ibadan-born women.

388. Awosika, K. (1986) Women in Urban Labour Force: Implications for Manpower Planning in Nigeria. In F. Ojo, A. Aderinto, & T. Fashoyin (eds.), Manpower Development and Utilization in Nigeria: Problems and Policies. Lagos: Lagos University Press.

This study seeks to identify the major socioeconomic transformation variables that affect modification of traditional childbearing practices. The results revealed that female employment has no effect on fertility. Employed women who presumably should have more role conflict with the demands of motherhood have a higher fertility rate than women who are unpaid family workers. The paper suggests that this negative association could be that women in predominantly illiterate societies in the process of transition receive adequate mechanisms for adjusting the traditional beliefs in large families to the demands of urban employment, that is, extended family help and hired househelpers.

389. Awosika, K. (1981) Women's Education and Participation in the Labour Force: The Case of Nigeria. In M. Rendel (ed.), Women, Power and Political Systems. London: Croom Helm Press.

The definition of labour force participation and the attending yardstick to measure it in developing countries, in relation to Nigeria, are examined. Supported by statistics, the paper reveals that there is the tendency for women in employment in Nigeria to be crowded around the lower rungs of the employment ladder due to the fact that a majority of them do not possess a university education. The author suggests adequate educational provisions be undertaken for women to participate effectively in development and for more research into inhibiting factors to active participation of women in development.

390. Benson, S., & Duffield, M. (1979) Women's Work and Economic Change: The Hausa in Sudan and in Nigeria. *Institute of Development Studies Bulletin*.

University of Sussex, Brighton, 10(9), June, 13-19.

A comparative study of women's economic roles between Hausa women in Nigeria and Sudan. The Paper reveals that Hausa women in Nigeria have moved from spinning and weaving to embroidery of men's caps and food vendoring. While their counterparts in Sudan, because of capitalism and mechanised agriculture, are becoming more economically dependent on their husbands.

391. Chineme, P.O. (1991) Women in the Labour Force: Problems and Prospects. Paper presented at the International Conference on Women by the Institute of Education, University of Nigeria, Nsukka, 8-12 October.

The problems of combining work and family life reduce women's efficiency and productivity in either sphere. Because of these problems, a large number of women are neither very good civil servants nor are they the best of mothers. This paper takes a look at the special problems of working mothers and offers recommendations towards their amelioration.

392. Denga, D.I. (1983) Cultural Influences and Career Perception of Women in Nigeria. *Journal of the Institute of Educational and Vocational Guidance for Girls in Pakistan.*

393. DiDomenico, C.H., & Asun, Judith B. (1979) Breastfeeding Practices Among Urban Women in Ibadan, Nigeria. In D. Raphael, (ed.), *Breast-feeding and Food Policy in a Hungry World.* New York: Academic Press.

This study is based on an investigation conducted among 468 Yoruba working mothers in Ibadan, who had children under six years of age. The results revealed that only women in modern socioeconomic positions stopped breast-feeding babies of less than three months and that the majority stop breast-feeding when the infant is six months to one year of age. Only four out of 399 continued breast-feeding after one year. Half of the respondents preferred to use house helps, while only about one third preferred to leave their children in the care of relatives.

394. DiDomenico, C.H., & Lacey-Mojeetan, L. (1977) Occupational Status of Women in Nigeria: A Comparison of Two Urban Centres. *Africana*

Marbugensia, 10(2), 62-79.

This study was conducted at Ibadan and Kano cities using a total of 1,086 and 777 women from the two cities respectively. The proportion participating in the labour force in Ibadan rose progressively from 65 percent in the 20 to 29 year old age group to 89 percent among those in the 50 to 59 year old age group; while in Kano the proportion ranged between 27.5 percent and 53.3 percent for the two cohorts. There is a differing acquisition of educational and occupational skills among the Hausa and Yoruba. Women in the two cities are far behind males in educational and occupational attainment.

395. Di Domenico, C.H. et al. (1977) Changing Status of African Women: An Explanatory Study of Working Mothers in Ibadan, Nigeria. In F.T. Sai (ed.), *Family Welfare and Development in Africa.* London: IPPF.

The results revealed that market women and craftswomen still cared for their small children in their places of work, while those in the modern sector rely on household and relatives to care for their children. Mothers working in the modern sector are not satisfied with this arrangement. Establishment of day-care centres was acceptable to both groups. This is suggested to help promote greater involvement of women in the labour force.

396. Duruamaku, E.E. (1991) Rhetorics of Women Education: The Experience of Rural Young Women Entrepreneurs in Cross River State. Paper presented at the International Conference on Women by the Institute of Education, University of Nigeria, Nsukka, 8-12 October.

Recently, Nigerian women showed increased interest in private enterprise enhanced by the establishment of such programmes as 'Otu Olu Obodo' and Better Life Programme for Rural Women. This empirical research paid special attention to rural young Nigerian women entrepreneurs. It established reasons for their involvement in entrepreneurship, identified types of business and inherent problems, and assessed prospects.

397. Fadayomi, T.O., et al (1977) The Role of Working Mother in Early Childhood Education: A Nigerian Case Study. Final Report to UNESCO Through the Federal Ministry of Education.

Seven states were studied with a sample of 790 working mothers with pre-school children. The characteristics of the women were provided. A majority of the women were self-employed, followed by civil servants. The major reason for working was economic necessity. A greater number of the working mother's children were cared for by relatives.

398. Fatunla, G.T. (1991) Women Education and Entrepreneurship in Nigeria. Paper presented at the International Conference on Women by the Institute of Education, University of Nigeria, Nsukka, 8-12 October.

The proportion of women entrepreneurs in Nigeria is very low indeed. The paper uses statistics to show that in the few cases where women own enterprises, they are usually in petty trading, arts/crafts, and cottage industries requiring mainly traditional technologies where productivity and income are low. These categories of businesses are also characterised by a low capital base. The paper discusses women's limited access to credit from banks and other institutional financial sources. It also discusses how a low level of education is the major factor responsible for the low proportion of women entrepreneurs. Their abilities are constrained when producing products/services that require modern technology, large capital-base, high management, and marketing skills.

399. Fapohunda, E.R. (1978) Characteristics of Women Workers in Lagos. *Labour and Society*, 3(2) 158-171.

400. Idowu, L. (1986) The Attitude of Market Women in Lagos Metropolis to Small-Sized Families: A Case Study of Balogun, Oshodi and Tejuosho Markets. *Unpublished M.Ed. Thesis*. Department of Education, University of Lagos, Lagos, Nigeria.

401. Ijere, M.O. (1991) Mobilising Womanpower for Nigeria's Economic Development. In M.O. Ijere (ed.), *Women in Nigerian Economy*. Enugu: Acena Publisher, 7-12.

This paper seeks to analyse the particular place and role of trained woman power, the lack of encouragement, the opposition from the menfolk, and the reluctance of women to take up management positions.

402. Ijere, M.O. (1989) Women in Small-Scale Industrial Cooperatives: Relief to Urban Migration. In M.O. Ijere (ed.), *Women in Nigerian Cooperatives*.Centre for Rural Development and Cooperatives, U.N.N., 17-32.

403. Jackson, S. (1978) Hausa Women on Strike. *Review of African Political Economy*, 13, 21-26.

This study is on the 150 women working for a Brussel-based company that grow and harvest vegetables in a Kano River Project. These women went on strike for higher wages and won. The factors that were responsible for the strike, in view of the fact that Hausa women are reputedly submissive, are: that this was a group of old, respected, highly opinionated and influential women in the community, and working outside the male-oriented structure gave them freedom to assert their needs.

404. Lucas, D. (1976) The Participation of Women in the Nigerian Labour Force Since the 1950s with Particular Reference to Lagos. *Unpublished Ph.D. Dissertation*. University of London.

405. Mpamugo, Ikedi (1989) Women and the Challenges of Management. Paper presented at the Management Workshop on Developing Women's Potentials in Management by Anambra State Branch of the Nigerian Institute of Management at Enugu, September.

406, Nnaka, C. (1991) Encouraging Women in Business Through Education. Paper presented at the International Conference on Women by the Institute of Education, University of Nigeria, Nsukka, 8-12 October.

Women's work covers every sector of the economy; women grow, process and market food, make goods, and provide services. But it often remains unpaid or under-valued. Given the conditions under which women work, any attempt to ameliorate their situation needs to be multifaceted. Intervention programmes should range from changing the policy environment to increasing their productivity through training, education, investment, improved technology, and improved institutional framework. This paper examines how some of these intervention programmes can help encourage more women into business, and how women's participation and productivity can be increased through education.

407. Nwoko, S.C. (1983) Analysing Multiple Occupational Activities: Case Studies of Idumuje-Ugboko Women of Bendel State, Nigeria. *West African Journal of Education,* XXIV (1-3), 44-50.

408. Obi, C. (1991) Socio-Psychological Skills that Influence the Success of Women Managers in the Banks. Paper presented at the International Conference on Women by the Institute of Education, University of Nigeria, Nsukka, 8-12 October.

Management is a relatively new field of employment for women. As a result, their number appears to be small when compared to the number of women in teaching and nursing professions. Research studies have revealed that the women in management positions encounter managerial problems more than their male counterparts. In spite of these problems, some women have succeeded and have continued to progress. It thus becomes necessary to find out from those who have succeeded the affective work skills that have helped them to succeed. A total of 113 female managers and their supervisors were surveyed. The questionnaire was used to collect the data that was analysed using frequency counts, percentages and mean scores. The one-way analysis of variance (ANOVA) was used to test for significant differences among managers in the three levels of management-operating, middle, and top management.

409. Odeyemi, O.O. (1991) Women as Food Scientists and Technologists in Nigeria. Paper presented at the International Conference on Women by the Institute of Education, University of Nigeria, Nsukka, 8-12 October.

This paper is making a case for women to be involved in food science and technology. Food scientist and technologists are those actively involved in food production, marketing, processing, preservation, and storage processes. Women involved in food science and technology are of two categories: those that belong to the informal sector and those in the formal wage-earning sector. Informal sector activities can be characterized as cottage-industries. These are limited to simple technologies and belong, in most cases, to the rural areas. The role of women in this sector is significant in that they form the root of Nigerian women who are making positive contributions to national development. The formal sector includes women in food industries, research institutes, institutions of higher learning, and government agencies. They have attained a certain level of education with National Diploma (ND) in Food Science and Technology. Women food scientists and technologists are in a better position to understand the responsibilities involved in the supply, distribution, and consumption of food to ensure the welfare of the individual, the family, the community, the nation, and the world.

410. Okafor, Laz (1991) Experience of Women in Science and Technology-Based Occupations in Nigeria. Paper presented at the International Conference on Women by the Institute of Education, University of Nigeria, Nsukka, 8-12 October.

Many Nigerian women have proven to be highly talented and an increasing number of them are in science and technology-based jobs. In spite of the increasing role and participation of these women in these disciplines, there is a need for greater participation in these areas. This paper addresses these issues.

411. Okojie, C.E.E. (1984) Female Migrations in the Urban Labour Market: Benin City, Nigeria. *Canadian Journal of African Studies*, 18(3), 547-562.

412. Okojie, C.E.E. (1982) Determinants of Labour Force Participation of Urban Women in Nigeria:A Case Study of Benin City, *Nigeria Journal of Economic and Social Studies*, 26(1).

This paper focuses on factors that affect women's participation in the labour force in a city in Nigeria. Some of the determining factors include education, number of children, and family income. Suggestions to improve the participation of women in the labour force in Nigeria were made.

413. Okwuosa, A.C. (1990) Igbo Women and Modernisation in a Peasant Economy. Paper presented at the Seminar on Igbo Women in Socioeconomic Change. Better Life Programme (Imo State Wing) Owerri/Institute of African Studies, University of Nigeria, Nsukka, 3-5 April.

This paper intends to demonstrate the fallacy of Roger's model of peasantry, as well as the sexist conception of peasant roles in socioeconomic development. The paper hypothesizes that among the Igbos of Nigeria, the men are not the key actors in developmental processes among peasants, and writings on peasant behaviour should really be conceived in terms of 'she'.

414. Olaitan, S.O. (1987) Child Custodianship in Ondo State and Its Policy Implications. Paper presented at the First Annual Conference of OMEP (Organisation for Early Childhood Education), University of Nigeria, Nsukka, 20-23 May.

The author laments that the problem of child-care while the mother is away at work is no longer that of the mother but of the state. Using 180 literate working mothers in the state, the necessary information was collected through a questionnaire. Means, percentages, and chi-square were applied to analyse the data. Some of the findings are that mothers combine their responsibility of child rearing with official work. Low socioeconomic status mothers make use of home help more than the high socioeconomic status mothers. Recommendations are made to alleviate the problems.

415. Onifade, A. (1977) Attitudes Towards Abortion in Ibadan. *Nigeria Medical Journal*.

This is a rejoinder to the 1973 study carried out by the author among women office and factory workers in Ibadan. Of the 90 women who reported having procured abortions, thirty-five said that the abortion was not spontaneous. Many of these women were single or in school. Support for legalized abortion was given only for abortion on medical grounds.

416. Onyema, C.N. (1989) Women in Labour Force: A Study of Anambra State Civil Service. *Unpublished MPA Thesis*. Sub-Department of Public Administration and OCA Government, University of Nigeria, Nsukka. 157pp.

The author intends to identify problems militating against the effective participation of women in the Anambra State civil services labour force vis-à-vis the hypothesis that women's biological constitution does not determine their effectiveness in the labour force. Some of the constraints identified include child bearing and child-care, family and marital problems, legal discrimination, prejudices, and biases based on tradition and culture. Most importantly, sex or biological constitutions had no effect on the women's work.

417. Osu, C.O. (1989) A Study to Compare the Work Value of Female and Male Managers in Industry: Implications for Tertiary Level Job Preparation. Paper presented at the Nigerian Vocational Association International Conference, University of Nigeria, Nsukka, 5-6 October.

418. Pearce, T.O. et al. (1988) Generating an Income in the Urban Environment: The Experience of Street Food Vendors in Ile-Ife, Nigeria. *Africa*, 58(4) 385-400.

419. Peil, M. (1975) Female Roles in West African Towns. In Goody, J. (ed.), *Changing Structure in Ghana*.

The author focuses on the interaction between economic and other roles in the lives of urban women using national and sample census and interviews collected from two Ghanaian and four Nigerian cities (Kaduna, Lagos, Abeokuta and Aba). The author concludes that participation in the labour force is a more important factor in a woman's marital life than in her social adjustment. This paper suggests that increased trading activity is more often the result rather than a cause of the loosening of the conjugal tie and hence associated with divorced or widowed women.

420. Porter, R.E. (1988) Perspectives on Trade, Mobility and Gender in a Rural Market System: Borno, Northeast Nigeria. *Tijdschrift voor Economische en Sociale Geografie*, 79(2), 82-92.

421. Ramy, D.C. (1975) Underdevelopment and the Experience of Women: A Nigerian Case Study. In R.R. Reither (ed.), *Toward an Anthropology of Women*. New York: Monthly Review Press.

This paper discusses the participation of 24 wives of Nigerian Tobacco Company workers in an indigenous economy. Hausa and non-Hausa women were compared with respect to the degree to which they were economically independent of their husbands or family, as well as the extent to which they were able to participate directly in the economic or social life of the community.

422. Schildkrout, E. (1980) Women and Children's Work in Urban Kano. In Sandra Wallman (ed.), *The Anthropology of Work*. London: Academic Press,

Association of Social Anthropologists, No. 9.

This paper examines the variations in Hausa women's economic roles and the factors which led to the occupational choices and income differentials such as age, class, marital status, child-bearing history and husband's occupation. Despite tremendous income differentials between women in the two wards, the women's socioeconomic positions were not directly affected because marriage was primarily used to define a woman's status.

423. Segynola, H.A. (1991) Female Leadership in Educational Administration in Nigeria: The Alele-Williams Phenomenon at the University of Benin, Benin City as a Case Study. Paper presented at the International Conference on Women by the Institute of Education, University of Nigeria, Nsukka, 8-12 October.

Little is known about leadership in higher education administration in Nigeria, particularly with reference to Nigerian university management. The paucity of documentated research in this area further heightens when viewed against the background of female leadership as a most recent phenomenon in the management of universities in Nigeria. Besides, studies known to this author on university administration have only concentrated on leadership in general. Thus, so far in this field, no attempt has been made to clearly distinguish the phenomenon of female leadership from the mainstream of leadership in Nigerian universities in studies carried out to date. In this study, the research investigated the contributions of Alele-Williams at the University of Benin, Benin City. The study also examines the problems and prospects of female leadership with particular reference to the management of Nigerian higher educational institutions. The study covers the period 1985 to 1991.

424. Standing, G., & Sheehan, G. (1978) Economic Activity of Women in Nigeria. In Standing, G. and Sheehan, G. (eds.), *Labour Force Participation in Nigeria*.

This study intends to identify whether formalization of economic activity has pushed women out of the labour force. A total of 2,700 women twenty years and over from socio-cultural environments represented by Lagos, Ibadan, and Zaria were used. The results reveal that lack of financial support leads to higher participation rates by women in both women's education and participation in the labour force. The paper concludes that urbanization could lead to marginalization of women in the labour force.

425. Sudarkasa, Niara (1981) Female Employment and Family Organisation in West Africa. In F.C. Stead (ed.), *The Black Woman Cross-Culturally*, Cambridge, Massachusetts: Schenkman Publishing Co., 49-63.

426. Trager, L. (1977) Market Women in the Urban Economy: The Role of Yoruba Intermediaries in a Medium-Sized City. *African Urban Notes*, 2(3), 1-10.

This paper discusses the central role played by Yoruba women traders in urban and regional economics. Women predominated in the bulk buying and resale of agricultural produce and in the retailing of manufactured goods. Despite this, their incomes were meagre, usually below the minimum wage and most of their incomes were spent meeting the immediate needs of feeding and caring for their families.

427. Udeogalanya, V.N. (1985) Factors that Motivate Female Labour Force Participation in Nigeria: A Case Study of Nsukka Town. *Unpublished M.Sc. Thesis*. Department of Economics, University of Nigeria, Nsukka, 103 pp.

The main objective of the study is to identify the reasons females work and also highlight the relationship between motives and personal characteristics of the females. The study also investigated the attitudes of males to female participation in the labour force. Results reveal that the major reasons females work are to be self-supporting, followed by the desire to have security. Of least importance are the motives to escape boredom and to have power and control, and/or prestige. Men's attitude to female participation in the labour force is positive in view of current economic realities in the country.

428. William, S.B. (1988) Women's Participation in the Fish Industry in Nigeria: A Review. In T.O. Adekanye (ed.) *Women in Agriculture, African Notes: Journal of Institute of African Studies*. Special No. 3, WORDOC, University of Ibadan, 45-48.

Approximately 73 percent of the labour force engaged in the processing, distribution, and marketing of fish products from traditional artisenal fisheries are women. Active participation of these women is aimed at supplementing the traditional fishermen's low income.

429. Wilson, E.B. (1984) Working Women and Care of the Young Child in Western Nigeria. *African Review,* 11(1), 56-67.

430. Zack-Williams, A.B. (1985) Female Urban Employment. In WIN (ed.), *Women in Nigeria Today.* London: Zed Book Ltd., 104-113.

This study is mainly concerned with the female construction worker of Jos Local Government Area of Plateau State in Nigeria. The paper is divided into seven sections: introduction, methodology, recruitment procedure, types of work and remuneration, workers reaction to workers insecurity, the views of the male workers, and conclusion. To overcome the over-exploitation of female labour within the industry, the state should change from exclusive to inclusive legislation in addition to a total transformation of Nigerian society.

7

General

431. Acholonu, R. (1989) Elechi Amadi's Positive Feminism: A Study of Estrangement. Paper presented at Elechi Amadi Symposium, University of Port Harcourt, 12-13 May.

The main thrust of the argument in this study is the attempt to differentiate between the positively and dynamically self-liberating feminism from the negatively and radically self-disorientating brand which tends to thrive on romanticised ideals, rather than on possible realities.

432. Ada, M.J. (1991) Women Education, Politics and Public Administration: The Case of Nigerian Women. Paper presented at the International Conference on Women by the Institute of Education, University of Nigeria, Nsukka, 8-12 October.

This paper aims at highlighting the historical growth of the Nigerian women in education, politics and public administration. Their roles as nation builders in this last decade of the 20th century are assessed.

433. Adam, W. (1989) The Role of Efik Women in Calabar 1850's to the 1950's. *Unpublished B.A Thesis.* Department of History, University of Calabar, Calabar.

434. Adelabu, M.A. (1991) Politics, Education and Women in Educational Leadership: An Historical Perspective. Paper presented at the International Conference on Women by the Institute of Education, University of Nigeria, Nsukka, 8-12 October.

This study investigated politics of Nigerian education since the colonial era, highlighting its influence on women education in general and educational leadership in particular. The study reviewed the historical antecedents of the politics of the traditional educational system, and the missionary colonial educational politics as they affect women. Furthermore, the study also investigated the present status of women in educational leadership focusing on

Oyo state secondary school principalship. The study methodology involved collection of archival records and literature. Questionnaires were administered on some Oyo state principals and school board members on the politics behind the appointment of principals. The findings of the study sheds more light on how policy makers, as far as politics and women's education are concerned, have consistently linked the present with the historical past.

435. Achebe, C. (1990) Myth and Power: The Hidden Power of Igbo Women. In R. Granquist (ed.), *Travelling: Chinua Achebe in Scandinavia*. Umea, Sweden.

436. Afigbo, A.E. (1991) Women in Nigerian History. In M.O. Ijere (ed.), *Women in Nigerian Economy*. Enugu: Acena Publishers, 22-40.

The author gives a panoramic view of the steps through which Nigerian women have risen in the social ladder, contrasting post-independent with pre-colonial and colonial periods of the country. The author debunks a lot of misconceptions about women which foreign and indigenous writers like to parody.

437. Afigbo, A.E. (1990) Igbo Women, Colonialism and Socioeconomic Change. Paper presented at a Seminar on Igbo Women in Socioeconomic Change. Better Life Programme (Imo State Wing), Owerri/ Institute of African Studies,, University of Nigeria, Nsukka, 3-5 April.

Colonialism is seen as a movement that generally led to the relegation of women either as active agents helping to inaugurate, define, and manage change or as passive agents receiving and adapting to change. The paper further discussed women and political, economic, and social changes, and Igbo women, colonialism, and change. The author concludes that Igbo womanhood emerged from colonialism as a more purposive force, making for socioeconomic change.

438. Ajayi-Obe, P.C. (1985) Inequality and Infringement of Rights of Nigerian Women. Paper presented at the Seminar on Nigerian Women and National Development, Institute of African Studies, University of Ibadan, 20-12 June.

This study points out that although Nigerian women have been empowered by the Women's Property Law, which is similar to the 1892 Women's Property Act of England to own property, this is not put into practice. Women lawyers have been called upon to work hard towards the total elimination of any existing laws that tended to discriminate against or infringe upon the rights of women, and towards carrying out the Women's Property Law to the letter.

439. Akande, J.O. (1979) Law and the Status of Women in Nigeria. Economic Commission for Africa/African Training and Research Centre for Women. ECA/A TRCW/RE 801/79.

This paper criticises the Nigerian law, which although it favours women on paper, tradition and culture deny women the enjoyment of the law. This is especially true in the areas of marital and family life as well as employment. The forceful criticisms of the paper could be said to be consequent to elimination of some provisions of Nigerian law that discriminated against women from the Nigerian Constitution adopted in October, 1979.

440. Amechi, E.E. (1979) The Legal Status of Nigerian Women with Special Reference to Marriage. *Unpublished Ph.D. Dissertation.* Faculty of Law, SOAS, University of London.

This thesis is an indepth study of the law and the Nigerian women. Areas covered are family and marriage, women and customary marriage and its dissolution, polygamy and status of women, western form of marriage and its effect on women, property rights, and rights to succession, among others. Useful statistical data on the educational, occupation, marital and divorce characteristics of women were also provided.

441. Amechi, E.E. (1976) The Legal Rights of Women in Nigeria in Relation to the Law of Property. *A Year to Remember.* International Women's Year Committee, University of Nigeria, Nsukka, 58-97.

The author examined the existing laws/regulations and practices in Nigeria and pinpointed where they are discriminatory, unfair, and unjust to women in regard to right of acquisition, holding disposal, and inheritance of property. Suggestions were proffered as to how to modify, and amend or totally abolish such laws/regulations to the benefit of the women, the family, and the country.

442. Amosu, Akwe (1987) Everyday Atrocities. *West Africa*, London: May 4, 860-861.

This paper calls for an end to the silence regarding the truth of men's violence against women in Nigeria, despite the effort of Women in Nigeria (WIN) to break the silence.

443. Amuta, Chidi (1989) The Nigerian Woman as a Dramatist: The Instance of Tess Onwueme. In H. Otokunefer and Obiageli Nwodo (eds.), *Nigerian Female Writers - A Critical Perspective*. Lagos: Malthouse Press Ltd.

444. Anozie, F.N. (1990) Igbo Women in Socioeconomic Change: Some Archaeological and Historical Evidence. Paper presented at the Seminar on Igbo Women in Socioeconomic Change. Better Life Programme (Imo State Wing) Owerri/Institute of African Studies, University of Nigeria, Nsukka, 3-5 April.

This paper relies on archaeological and oral historical evidence to reconstruct the position of Igbo women in various periods of Igbo history. The author, however, observes that evidence concerning women in the excavated archaeological sites in Igboland are very scanty. Partly because very few sites have been excavated and partly because archaeological data are never complete for obvious reasons.

445. Aronson, Lisa (1984) Women in the Arts. In Margaret Jean Hay & Sharon Stichter (eds.). *African Women South of the Sahara*. London and New York: Longman, 119-138.

The write-up begins with a discussion of the boundaries dividing women's from men's arts. It also examined factors explaining their existence and how they become blurred or redefined. Also discussed were the arts that women perform in terms of their domestic orientation using weaving and wall-painting. The art of pottery was used to illustrate the socioeconomic function of women. In conclusion, the author looked at how change in society affects change in women's arts and how they adapt to the shifts in their economy brought about by new trading patterns.

446. Arousi, M.E. (1977) Judicial Dissolution of Marriage. *Journal of Islamic*

and Comparative Law, Vol. 7, 13-20.

This paper examines the five situations in which marriage may be judicially dissolved according to *Sunna and Hanafi, Malikis* and the *Hanbalis* schools of Islamic jurisprudence of Sharia. The paper does not subscribe to the transfer of the powers to dissolve marriage from the husband to the judge.

447. Babatope, B. (1987) Women of our Society with Emphasis on Economic and Political Problems Facing Women of Southern Nigeria. *Presence Africaine*, No. 141, 15-28.

This discussion on Nigerian women highlights the following topics: their heritage, in the colonial era, in the first and second republics, in commerce and bureaucracy, social culture, and challenges for the future.

448. Badejo, B. (1990) Nigeria Women's Quest for Political Leadership in the Third Republic, *Nigerian Forum*, 10(3&3) March/April, Nigerian Institute of International Affairs, Lagos, 80-90.

The concern of this paper is to understand why women in Nigeria have been relegated to the background with respect to overt participation in political activities. The paper analyses the problem of under-representations of women in public office. Women are advised to organise themselves beyond the coming together of a few well-placed women, to including the greater majority of women who reside in the rural areas.

449. Boyd, T., & Last, M. (1985) The Role of Women as Agents Religieuz' in Sokoto. *Canadian Journal of African Studies*, 19(2), 283-300.

450. Callaway, B.J. (1987) Women and Political Participation in Kano City. *Comparative Politics*, 19(4), 379-393.

451. Callaway, B.J. (1984) Ambiguous Consequences of the Socialization and Seclusion of Hausa Women. *Journal of Modern African Studies*, 22(3), September, 429-450.

452. Callaway, B.J., & Kleeman, K.E. (1985) Three Women of Kano: Modern Women and Traditional Life. *African Report*, 30(2), 26-29.

453. Cobham-Sander, R. (1986) Class vs Sex: The Problem of Values in the Modern Nigerian Novel. *The Black Scholar*, 17(4), July/August 17-27 (Oakland, California).

This paper concludes that Nigerian women writers need to question the function of education within the Third World, the consequences of affluence, and the implications of the nuclear family. They will then be able to communicate their need for a better deal for women and will be able to incorporate a critique of their own roles as female members of a privileged elite.

454. Chineme, P.O., and Azikiwe, U. (1991) Women's Access to Property Ownership Under Nigerian Marriage Laws and Customs: Implications for Women's Rights Policy. Research funded by Social Science Council of Nigeria through Ford Foundation Grant.

A sample of 239 married women were used for the study. The results revealed that married women are aware of marriage laws and customs as they affect their access to property ownership, but are unaware of laws that are in their favour. Property owned by the women include apparel, livestock, economic trees and so forth. Furthermore, it was revealed that tradition, religion, and duality of marriage prevent women from taking advantage of the provisions of the law. It was recommended that laws and customs which are reprehensible should be abrogated and enacted in a decree.

455. Chukwuma, F.C. (1991) Effectiveness: Strategies and Coping Skills for Female Leadership in Schools. Paper presented at the International Conference on Women by the Institute of Education, University of Nigeria, Nsukka, 8-12 October.

Increased participation of the women folk in the management of schools is a trend that is likely to continue into the 21st century. This study identified the needed strategies and coping skills for women to enable them to successfully manage schools in spite of their demanding gender-related roles and dispositions. The implications of the implementation of these strategies and coping skills are discussed.

456. Coker, F. (1987) *A Lady: A Biography of Lady Oyinkan Abayomi*. Lagos: Evans Brothers (Nig.) Ltd., 111pp.

This book chronicled the life and long career of Lady Abayomi who successfully combined her teaching career with her duties as a wife. Her contributions to the promotion of education of girls and especially her leading role in the development of Queen's School, Lagos, were presented in detail. She was a social worker and was instrumental to the establishment of the Girls Guides Association which she led from 1951 to 1962. In the political sphere, she was once a Lagos Town Councillor and in 1944 founded the first Women's Party.

457. Dangogo, H.S. (1985) Women in Electronic Media. In WIN (ed.), *Women in Nigeria Today*. Zed Book Ltd., 208-211.

This paper attempts to throw more light on the type of duties women are made to carry out in the media and how far they have gone in working their way up to the management cadre.

458. Denzer, L. (1989) Women in Colonial Nigerian History: An Appraisal. Paper presented at the Symposium on the Impact of Colonialism on Nigerian Women. Institute of African Studies, University of Ibadan, 16-19 October.

459. Ebo, S.J. (1989) The Image of the Nigerian Woman in the Electronic Media. *Unpublished M.A. Thesis*. Department of Mass Communication, University of Nigeria, Nsukka, 94 pp.

This study examines the commercial content of the electronic media (radio, television, and films) to determine the extent of complimentary and non-complimentary roles played by women in the various facets of the media. The study found that there are not enough programmes that cover women's interests and activities because the media in Nigeria is male-dominated.

460. Eghobamien, A. (1985) The Role of the Nigerian Women in the Professions. *Nigerian Forum,* 5(9 and 10), The Nigerian Institute of

International Affairs. September/October, 229-233.

This paper discussed the role of Nigerian women in the social, economic, political, and other spheres of life. It further highlighted the contributions of women to development in Nigeria. It concluded by warning that the power of women in Nigeria should not be underestimated for future progress.

461. Ekpo. T.N. (1991) Managerial Stress Among Women in Education, Politics and Public Administration. Paper presented at the International Conference on Women by the Institute of Education, University of Nigeria, Nsukka, 8-12 October.

In this study, a standardized questionnaire on stress was used to survey the sources, levels, and symptoms of stress from a random sample of women in three professions. The result of one-way ANOVA confirmed a significant difference in the sources, levels, and symptoms of stress in the three professions the women are engaged in. The implications are discussed.

462. Emeagwali, G.T. (1985) Women in Pre-Capitalist Socioeconomic Formations in Nigeria. In WIN (ed.) *Women in Nigeria Today*. London: Zed Book Ltd., 52-55.

The author states that the "women" question is fundamentally related to the infrastructural conditions and environment at specific periods in the transformation of the production process. In the course of the paper, a few observations vis-à-vis historiography and the period in question are made. Specific comments are given on the issue of the activities of women in precapitalist socioeconomic formations that existed in Nigeria before the nineteenth century. A great part of the paper is conjectural for reasons discussed in the initial part of the paper.

463. Emenanjo, E.N. (1987) Women as Traditional Rulers: The Omu Society Among the West Niger Igbo. Paper presented at the workshop on Women in Igbo Society, University of Nigeria, Nsukka, 28-31 October.

464. Ezenwa-Ohaeto (1987) Conservatism, Liberationism and Adversity: Reactions of Igbo Women to War Situations in Six Short Stories by Achebe,

Nwapa and Aniebo. Paper presented at the University of Nigeria, Nsukka, November.

This paper uses six short stories by the three Nigerian authors to portray the various reactions of Igbo women to war situations. The paper illustrates that while some women could rise beyond the mundane adverse conditions to become useful to the society, others tend to pursue the line of less resistance in acquiring material possessions and the basic necessities of life. The paper therefore establishes that the war short stories cast insight into the importance of understanding women in war situations.

465. Federal Republic of Nigeria (1989) Nigeria Country Paper: Problems, Programmes, Constraints and Recommendations. Report presented at the 4th Regional Conference on the Integration of Women in Development on the Implementation of the Arusha Strategies for the Advancement of Women in Africa, Abuja, Nigeria, 6-10 November.

This paper, being the country paper for the implementation of the Arusha Strategies, highlights the achievements of the Nigerian women since the declaration of the UN decade with emphasis on the progress since 1984 when the Arusha Strategies were articulated for the African Region. The paper also highlights the constraints to effective implementation of the Arusha Strategies. The activities of women organisations in Nigeria were discussed and recommendations were made.

466. HRC Old Girls Association (1989) Nigerian Womanhood: Past, Present and Future.

This booklet is a compilation of contributions of four branches of the association. The papers focus on the traditional roles of women per their status, the present day woman, positive and negative effects of education on her role in development, as well as the promises of a better future.

467. Ifionu, A.O. (1990) Igbo Women in Music and Drama. Paper presented at a Seminar on Igbo Women in Socioeconomic Change. Better Life Programme (Imo State Wing) Owerri/Institute of African Studies, University of Nigeria,

Nsukka, 3-5 April.

This paper makes a brief survey of Igbo women who have distinguished themselves in the field of music and drama/novel, considering both social and economic factors that militate against or promote their efforts. The ideological postures of the dramatists and novelists vis-à-vis their male counterparts are highlighted.

468. Ikpeze, N. (1990) Women in the Political Economy of Igboland. Paper presented at a Seminar on Igbo Women in Socioeconomic Change. Better Life Programme (Imo State Wing) Owerri/Institute of African Studies,, University of Nigeria, Nsukka, 3-5 April.

This paper discusses the issue in three parts: problems of applying the political economy approach to the situation of women in Igboland; problems of linkage between the role of women and their status in society with respect to political economy; and in view of the conclusions arising from the discussion of the first two parts, the third part is on policy making.

469. Jackson, S. (1978) Hausa Women on Strike. *Review of African Political Economy*, 13, 21-36.

470. Johnson, C. (1981) Madam Alimotu Pelewura and the Lagos Market Women. *Tarikh*. 7(1), 1-10.

471. Kale, M.O. (1985) The Role of Radio in Enhancing the Participation of Illiterate and Semi-Illiterate Women in Non-Formal Education Programmes in Oyo State. *Unpublished M.Ed. Thesis*. Department of Education, University of Ibadan, Ibadan, Nigeria.

472. Kalu, O.U. (1990) Gender Ideology in Igbo Religion: The Changing Religious Role of Women in Igboland. Paper presented at a Seminar on Igbo Women in Socioeconomic Change. Better Life Programme (Imo State Wing) Owerri/Institute of African Studies, University of Nigeria, Nsukka, 3-5 April.

This study is on the ambiguities, complexities, and changing perception of women's religious roles in Igboland. The paper concludes that in spite of ambiguities made, ascendancy in gender ideology has persisted at the religious level because women have not tapped the resources of biblical kerygma since neither traditional religion nor Islam holds any hopes for them.

473. Kirk, I. (1986) 'Women's War' or 'Aba riots'? A New Perspective on the Events in Southern Nigeria, 1929. *Folk*, 28, 61-87.

474. Kisekka, M.N. (1981) Women and Development in Nigeria: Bibliography Series No. 41. UNECA/ATRCN.

The bibliographical entries of 122 pages cover works on women up until 1981. The compilation was grouped into ten sub-sections. General studies; sex and puberty rites; marriage and the family; fertility and family planning; health; education; work and employment; law and politics and religion.

475. Maduewesi, E.J. (1980) Self-Esteem: A Psychological Dimension of Female Socialization. In F.I.A. Omu, P.K. Makinwa, and A.O. Ozo (eds.), *Proceedings of the National Conference on Integrated Rural Development and Women in Development*. Vol II, 877-885.

476. Mba, Nina (1990) Igbo Women and Politics (Nationalist and Post Colonial). Paper presented at a Seminar on Igbo Women in Socioeconomic Change. Better Life Programme (Imo State Wing) Owerri/Institute of African Studies, University of Nigeria, Nsukka, 3-5 April.

The author presents a historical survey of the activities of women in politics from colonial times to date. Women are advised to form associations and not to let political parties marginalise them into an ancillary women's wing.

477. Mba, Nina (1982) Nigerian Women Mobilized: Women's Political Activity in Southern Nigerian 1900-1965.

478. Mere, Ada (1976) Status of Igbo Women. A Year to Remember. International Women's Year Committee, University of Nigeria, Nsukka, 30-45.

This paper is an attempt to analyse the conflicts resulting from changes in the life of Igbo women due to the influence of Christianity and other western influences. The traditional status of Igbo women, complex and intricately interwoven into the fabric of Igbo social structures, derives from a number of fundamental social factors: child betrothal, polygyny, system of dowry, patriliny, patrilocal residence, motherhood, and familial role. The author's solution to improve the status of Igbo women is a multifaceted approach, using some of the social institutions and kin network, being involved in politics as a pressure group, pressing for policy choices, and the introduction of an awareness forum.

479. Mgbodile, T.O. (1991) Women and Management Positions in Primary and Secondary Schools. Paper presented at the International Conference on Women by the Institute of Education, University of Nigeria, Nsukka, 8-12 October.

The present trend, which shows the gradual withdrawal and disengagement of men from teaching in primary and post-primary institutions in many states of Nigeria, and the emergence and dominance of women in these places, calls for a realistic curricula programme that will prepare women to effectively play the inevitable role of running schools without men. This paper looks at women as future leaders and managers of schools and examines the problems likely to arise from this position, and how these are likely to affect the Nigerian educational system. The paper prescribes some management hints and strategies to cope with the situation.

480. Mohammed, H.D. (1985) Women in Nigerian History: Examples from Borno Empire, Nupeland and Igboland. In WIN (ed.), *Women in Nigeria Today*. London: Zed Books Ltd., 45-51.

The purpose of this paper is to present the role of women and their ability to do as men can do, especially in regard to what they have done in history. The paper buttressed this viewpoint by taking examples of women in Nigerian history. The examples are from the Borno Empire, where women are known to have organised the internal structures of the palace and its connection with state organisation; from Hausaland where Queen Amina had considerable successes in wars; and from Igboland and Nupeland where women are known to have played important roles in the political lives of their communities despite the patrilineal system of those societies.

481. Mohammed, S.I. (1991) Women in Educational Management in Northern States of Nigeria. Paper presented at the International Conference on Women by the Institute of Education, University of Nigeria, Nsukka, 8-12 October.

In the Northern states of Nigeria, the participation of women in educational management is relatively small compared to men. This paper attempts to examine the role conflict experienced by female educational managers in the Northern states of Nigeria.

482. Mustapha, A.R. (1985) On Combating Women's Exploitation and Oppression in Nigeria. In WIN (ed.), *Women in Nigeria Today*. London: Zed Books Ltd., 241-246.

The author outlines various dimensions of the subjugation of women namely: ideological, economic, and force (physical or psychological), which are closely related in real life. The paper laments that women have not done much to combat their subjugation. The author suggests that women should ally with other democratic forces in society to fight for their emancipation.

483. Nnabue, P. (1991) Nigerian Women as Executives in Social Service Institutions. Paper presented at the International Conference on Women by the Institute of Education, University of Nigeria, Nsukka, 8-12 October.

The success or failure of any human enterprise depends largely on effective management procedures, competencies, expertise, and experiences of the executives. A positive stance is being advocated by this writer in relation to the challenge of defining the appropriate roles Nigerian women can play in the management of social service institutions. This paper essentially examines, analyses, and provides some implications for practitioners, policy analysts, and planners. This paper focuses on the following: Nigerian women in educational management, distribution of Nigerian women in public service institutions, styles of management among women, some problems experienced by Nigerian women managers, and alternatives for improvement.

484. Nnolim, C. (1987) Mythology and the Unhappy Woman in Nigerian Fiction. In E.N. Emenyonu (ed.), *Critical Theory and African Literature,*

Ibadan: Heinemann, 45-53.

485. Nwachukwu, D. (1991) A Survey on Contemporary Elite Nigerian Christians on Women Participation in the Church. *Amka*, Issue No. 1. An occasional newsletter of the Biennial Institute of African Women in Religion and Culture. 72-75.

This paper empirically validated the opinions of 110 subjects on the concept and role of women in modern churches. Since women are subordinate to men, they are therefore excluded in performance of rituals to gods. Their roles in the church include sweeping, wardens or sides women, reading Bible lessons, Sunday School teachers, and so forth. Some of the constraints are highlighted.

486. Nwapa, F. (1987) Women in Politics. *Presence Africaine*, No. 141, 1st Quarterly, 115-121.

This paper discusses the role of women in the presidential system of government in Nigeria. The author is of the view that the Nigerian women can and should influence the presidential system of politics.

487. Nweke, T. (1985) The Role of Women in Nigerian Society: The Media. In WIN (ed.), *Women in Nigeria Today*. London: Zed Books Ltd., 210-207.

The author argues that women in Nigeria have no place in the social structure. The attitude towards women in the society is to humour, to tolerate, not to take seriously, not to behave as if both parties have equal rights, since she is inherently inferior, she is only a woman. In the media, the progress of women is marginal and tokenistic, not only in Nigeria, but also in the developed countries. The paper suggests that to better the lots of women, traditional male attitudes must be ventilated, examined, and changed. On the other hand, women should be self-reliant, as this is the first step to freedom.

488. Nwogugu, E.I. (1976) The Position of Women in the Changing Family Law in Nigeria. *A Year to Remember*. International Women's Year Committee, University of Nigeria, Nsukka. 98-113.

This paper discussed the traditional customary marriage and the ordinance marriage introduced by the colonial masters. The advantages and disadvantages of these two types of marriages contracted in Nigeria were highlighted. It is brought to light that Nigeria, in 1970, enacted her own laws on matrimonial causes -- the Matrimonial Cause Decree. The paper in the final analysis advocated for one law to regulate the incidence of all marriages irrespective of whether they are monogamous or polygamous. The new law will jettison the old ones that are oppressive to women. The paper enjoined women to be ready to play a part, which is being aware of the laws and rights, and the readiness to utilize them.

489. Obadina, E. (1985) How Relevant is the Western Women's Liberation Movement for Nigeria? In WIN (ed.), *Women in Nigeria Today*. London: Zed Books Ltd., 138-142.

The author sums up what the women's liberation movement (WLM) is. It is women's struggle to liberate themselves from the shackles of domesticity and to have equal opportunity in determining their future. Nigerian women, according to the paper, constitutionally have all the rights Western women have had to battle for decades to obtain. However, there is clearly a crying need for improvements in the lives of the majority of Nigerian women. In view of the fact that Nigeria's womenfolk may emulate WLM of the West, the paper highlights some of the pitfalls of such an approach.

490. Obafemi, Olu (1989) Zulu Sofola's Theatre. In H. Otokunefer & Obiageli Nwodo (eds.), *Nigerian Female Writers-A Critical Perspective*. Lagos: Malthouse Press Ltd.

491. Ogbuagu, S. (1983) Depro Provera-A Choice or an Imposition on the African Woman: A Case Study of Depro Provera Usage in Maiduguri. *African Review*, 10(2), 39-51.

492. Okadigbo, C. (1988) Gender Representatives in the Nigerian Press. Paper presented at the IAMCR Conference, Barcelona, Spain.

493. Okadigbo, M. (1977) Discrimination Provision in the Draft Constitution: Two Points of Dissent. Paper presented at the Political Science Symposium.

A criticism of the draft constitution with reference to Islamic laws and the rights of women. The paper objects to the operation of the Sharia court system alongside the judicial system.

494. Okaro, E.N. (1976) The Role of Women in Broadcasting. *A Year to Remember.*International Women's Year Committee, University of Nigeria, Nsukka, 114-119.

The author discusses the role of women at home to make the work of all broadcasters (inform, educate, entertain) more effective in the society. Women are advised not to be passive listeners but rather to be critical and analytical.

495. Okonjo, K. (1990) A Question of Group Survival: The Social Roles of Women in Igbo Society. Paper presented at a Seminar on Igbo Women in Socioeconomic Change. Better Life Programme (Imo State Wing) Owerri/Institute of African Studies, University of Nigeria, Nsukka, 3-5 April.

The author gave a brief sketch of the institutions and activities of Igbo Women in pre-colonial, colonial, and post-colonial periods of Igbo history. The paper concluded that Igbo women and their institutions have been a force for ensuring the continued existence of the Igbo as a group. They have ensured that the basic characteristics of Igbo society have been maintained, such as the predominance of group values, the communalistic societal structure, ideology of solidarity of the group, and the relative lack of gender bias in society.

496. Okonjo, K. (1981) Women's Political Participation in Nigeria. In F.C. Stead (ed.), *The Black Women Cross-Culturally*, Cambridge, Massachusetts: Schenkman Publishing Company, 99-107.

497. Okonjo, Kamene (1976) The Dual-Sex Political System in Operation: Igbo Women and Community Politics in Midwestern Nigeria. In N.J. Hotkin & E.G. Bay (eds.), *Women in Africa: Studies in Social and Economic Change.* California: Stanford University Press, 45-58.

This paper described the dual-sex political system that existed among those Igbo who live west of the Niger River before the coming of the colonial masters. It further assessed the effects of colonial rule and social change upon the system.

The author laments that modern political roles are supposed to be 'sex-blind', yet the absence of women from meaningful political representation in independent Nigeria is an indication of the legacy of single-sex politics the British colonial masters left behind.

498. Okonjo, Kamene (1977) Some Methodological Problems in the Conduct of Women Studies Among the Rural Igbo of Nigeria. Paper presented at the Workshop on Igbo Culture, University of Nigeria, Nsukka, 4-7 April.

This paper highlighted some of the constraints encountered by researchers who work on the rural women. Some of the constraints include illiteracy, hesitancy to give out information relating to age, and family life. The author makes suggestions that could make or mar successful research on rural women in Igboland.

499. Ola, V.U. (1982) The Christian Wives of John Munonye's Novels. *Okike*, No. 21, July.

500. Ola, V.U. (1978) The Portrayal of Women in West African Fiction with Special Emphasis on Nigerian Fiction. *Unpublished Ph.D. Dissertation*. Department of English, Zaria: Ahmadu Bello University.

501. Oladele, T. (1984) *Female Novelists of Modern Africa*. London: Macmillan Press.

502. Olusesi, M.A. (1987) Mass Media and Informal Education: The Role of Electronic Media in Family Planning. *Unpublished M.Ed. Thesis*. Department of Education, University of Ibadan, Ibadan, Nigeria.

503. Onunwa, U. (1989) Femininity in Igbo Cosmology: Paradoxes and Ambiguities. Paper presented at the Workshop on Igbo World View, Institute of African Studies, University of Nigeria, Nsukka, 3-6 December.

504. Osinulu, C. (1976) Religion and the Status of Nigerian Women. Paper presented at the National Conference on Nigerian Women and Development in Relation to Changing Family Structure, University of Ibadan, 26-30 April.

This paper examines the extent women are involved in religious rituals in Ibo, Efik, Yoruba and Hausa. Comparing Christianity and traditional religion, the paper observes that Christianity denied women rights to participate with the exception of indigenous churches, whereas traditional religion gave women almost equal status. Women in Islam have no part to play in that religion.

505. Oyeoku, O.K. (1990) Igbo Women and the Plastic Arts: Igbo Pottery Tradition. Paper presented at a Seminar on Igbo Women in Socioeconomic Change. Better Life Programme (Imo State Wing) Owerri/Institute of African Studies, University of Nigeria, Nsukka, 3-5 April.

This paper looks at the cultural values of Igbo pottery and the ways these values can be incorporated into modern techniques in order to enhance the status of the potters who are essentially women.

506. Pearse, A. (1978) Symbolic Characterization of Women in the Plays and Prose of Wole Soyinka. *Bashiru*, 9(1-2), 39-46.

507. Perchonock, N. (1985) Double Oppression: Women and Land Matters in Kaduna State. In WIN (ed.), *Women in Nigeria Today*. London: Zed Books Ltd., 82-103.

In the presentation of this paper, the author attempts to establish the class context of the oppression of women with regard to land matters in Kaduna State. The sources of oppression are the feudal local officials and the family system, hence, the double oppression. One solution suggests eliminating the feudal system through a process of basic democratization of village level political structures, a process in which women must play a full part. The position of women within the class system and the family system cannot improve as long as these feudal institutions continue to exist.

508. Pittin, R.I. (1985) Organising for the Future. In WIN (ed.), *Women in Nigeria Today*. London: Zed Books Ltd., 231-240.

This paper is of the view that change for the better with regards to subjugation and oppression of women is possible since 'no condition is permanent'. The change has to come through collective action, understanding, and strength.

Beliefs and practices that contribute to women's oppression must be identified, exposed, and ultimately eradicated.

509. Pittin, R.I. (1979) Hausa Women and Islamic Law: Is Reform Necessary? Paper presented to the 22nd Annual Meeting of the African Studies Association, Los Angeles, 31 October - 3 November.

This paper questions Islamic law using case studies of divorced women and court cases. This paper does not subscribe to reformation of the Islamic law, *talags*, with reference to dissolution of marriage and custody of children, which the author feels favour women.

510. Salamone, F.A. (1986) Religion and Repression Enforcing Feminine Inequality in an 'Egalitarian Society'. *Anthropos*, 81(4/6), 517-528.

The boundary identification importance of female purity in a South Italian community are extended to the Hune of Northern Nigeria. In both communities, religion is used to encapsulate and enforce the ideal of feminine chastity. Close examination reveals basic cultural and structural similarities between the two groups.

511. Sokoto, M.A. (1975) Prostitution as a Social Problem in the North Western State: Sabon-Gari, Sokoto Case Study. *Unpublished B.Sc. Thesis*. Department of Sociology, Zaria: Ahmadu Bello University.

This study investigated the lives of approximately 500 prostitutes in Sabon Gari as well as classified and analysed the different types of prostitution. Government's recognition of prostitution was condemned.

512. Staudt, K. (1977) The Characteristics of Women in Soyinka and Armah. *Bashiru*, 8(2), 63-69.

513. Ubagu, S. (1979) The Adaptation of Uli Motifs to Contemporary Igbo Women's Dress Patterns. *Unpublished MFA Thesis*. Department of Fine and Applied Arts, University of Nigeria, Nsukka, Nigeria.

The author attempts to investigate and compile a collection of Uli motifs used in Igboland and looks at the ways in which these are adapted to be incorporated into Igbo women's dress patterns. It also examines the design elements of Uli motifs, dress patterns, and comparisons made in order to analyse and find out how they affect each other. There are similarities between Uli motifs and motifs incorporated into dress patterns.

514. Ukpaukure, H. (1990) Woman in Man's World. *The Nigerian Economist,* 8(10).

515. Umeh, M. (1980) African Women in Transition in the Novels of Buchi Emecheta. *Presence Africaine,* No. 116, 190-201.

The author sees Buchi Emecheta's writings as the emergence of self-awareness feminism, women's liberation and the celebration of the black woman in a changing Nigerian society. Her stories centre around the extraordinary courage and resourcefulness of Nigerian women, which often prevents black families from disintegrating. In her attempt to propose change, she condemns the Nigerian males' insensitivity to the needs of their mothers, wives, sisters, and daughters.

516. Umoetuk, O.U. (1983) Clothing and Fashion in Ibibioland from Precolonial Times to 1980. *Unpublished Ph.D. Dissertation.* Department of Fine and Applied Arts, University of Nigeria, Nsukka, Nigeria.

This study examines the clothing and fashion habits of the Ibibio people as an aspect of their culture. More emphasis is placed on the female dress modes than the male dress style because women are regarded as the centre of attraction, and their clothing and fashion are more stimulating. The study reveals that there are different types of clothing and modes of dressing or fashion in Ibibio culture. The dress modes are a clear index of the advanced culture of the people, and the major consideration of Ibibio people in dress and fashion are in the aesthetics involving colour, pattern, and style.

517. Uwandu, D.N. (1987) The Child-Factor and the Image of Women in Igbo Drama. Paper presented at the 2nd annual Seminar on Igbo Life and Culture, University of Nigeria, Nsukka, 1-4 December.

This paper seeks to examine the child-factor as it affects women in Igbo drama from two perspectives: the image of the childless woman, and the image of the woman who has only female issues. In Igbo society, the woman is usually held responsible when any of the above situations arise. It is envisaged that this issue should be the concern of modern-day feminists, not as a matter of fighting for rights and privileges, but something they must let society understand as a human problem.

518. Uzoigwe, J. (1989) Igbo Women's Political Institutions. A Reassessment of the Impact of Colonialism. Paper presented at the Symposium on the Impact of Colonialism on Nigerian Women. Institute of African Studies, University of Ibadan, 16-19 October.

519. Van-Allen, J. (1975) Aba Riots or Igbo Women's War? *Ideology, Stratification and the Invisibility of Women,* 6(1), 11-39.

520. Van-Allen, J. (1976) Aba Riots or Igbo Women's War? ... Women in Africa: *Studies in Social and Economic Change.* Stanford: Stanford University Press.

An analysis of how Igbo women rioted in 1929 against colonial imposition of a native administration that destroyed the dual-sex political system. The introduction of Western education contributed more to the exclusion of women from political activities in their communities, as well as from participating in the modern economy. The author cites instances of women's participation in politics and the Biafran War and emphasizes that women's activism stems from Igbo tradition rather than from Western innovations.

521. Yusuf, B. (1985) Nigerian Women in Politics: Problems and Prospects. In WIN (ed.), *Women in Nigeria Today.* London: Zed Books Ltd., 212-216.

The author discussed the issue in three stages: the era of inactivity, the awakening, and the breakthrough. Each of these are characterized by certain peculiarities that differentiate it from the others. The solution to women's marginalization in politics is to encourage more women contest elections at all the levels-local government, state and national assemblies, especially the Senate where the major decisions are made and to seek to influence those decisions.

Author Index

Subject Index

Note: Numbers following subject names are entry numbers, not page numbers.

About the Compiler

UCHE AZIKIWE is Senior Lecturer of Education at the University of Nigeria.

ISBN 0-313-29960-9

HARDCOVER BAR CODE